# CREATIVE READING

## Grade 5

by

Lin Josephson

**Frank Schaffer Publications**®

Author: Lin Josephson
Editor: Rebecca Warren
Interior Designer: Lori Kibbey

## Frank Schaffer Publications®

Send all inquiries to:
Frank Schaffer Publications
3195 Wilson Drive NW
Grand Rapids, Michigan 49544

*The UnWorkbook: Creative Reading*—grade 5

ISBN: 0-7682-3125-6

1 2 3 4 5 6 7 8 9 10 PAT 10 09 08 07 06 05

# Table of Contents

The Eight Intelligences

 Verbal-Linguistic Intelligence

 Logical-Mathematical Intelligence

 Bodily-Kinesthetic Intelligence

 Visual-Spatial Intelligence

 Musical Intelligence

 Interpersonal Intelligence

 Intrapersonal Intelligence

 Naturalist Intelligence

# Standards Correlation Chart

| | Verbal–Linguistic Intelligence | Logical–Mathematical Intelligence | Bodily–Kinesthetic Intelligence | Visual–Spatial Intelligence | Musical Intelligence | Interpersonal Intelligence | Intrapersonal Intelligence | Naturalist Intelligence |
|---|---|---|---|---|---|---|---|---|
| **Main Ideas and Details:** | 8, 9, 11, 15 | 10, 15 | 8, 15 | 8, 9, 11, 12, 13 | 14 | 8, 10, 15 | 12, 14 | 11, 13 |
| **Prediction:** | 21, 22 | 17, 18, 19, 20, 22, 24 | 22 | 17, 18, 20 | | 18, 20, 21, 24 | | 16, 20, 23 |
| **Inference:** | 29, 31 | 25, 31, 33 | 25, 28, 29 | 27 | 26, 30 | 25, 29, 32, 33 | 27, 30, 32 | |
| **Summarization:** | 37, 39, 42 | 36, 41 | 34, 38, 40 | 35, 40 | | 34, 37, 39 | 38, 42 | 35 |
| **Sequence:** | 45, 49, 51 | 43, 44, 46, 48, 50, 51 | 47, 51 | 43, 45, 46, 50 | 49 | 43, 51 | 45 | |
| **Compare and Contrast:** | 60 | | 54 | 52, 54, 57 | 54, 55, 58, 60 | 52, 55, 57, 58, 59, 60 | 53, 56, 58 | 53, 56, 59 |
| **Cause and Effect:** | 65, 68 | 63, 66 | 63, 65, 69 | 62, 64, 67 | 66 | 61, 64, 68 | | 62, 67 |
| **Fact and Opinion:** | 72, 73 | | | 71, 74, 75, 76, 77, 78 | 75 | 70, 71, 72, 77 | 70, 74, 78 | 71, 76 |
| **Author's Purpose:** | 79, 85, 87 | 80, 81 | 79, 87 | | 82, 84, 86 | 84 | 83, 85 | 83, 85, 86 |
| **Story Elements:** | 89, 91, 95 | | 88, 89, 92, 93, 95 | 89, 90 | 89, 92, 94 | 93, 94, 95 | | 88, 90, 91, 95 |

0-7682-3125-6 *Creative Reading*

# Introduction

## Making the Best of Learning Styles

Imagine this book as a think tank for reading skills. The activities are imaginative, out of the box, and sometimes, a little wacky. There aren't any boundaries in this book. The premise is simple: since all students are individuals, it makes sense that they learn in different ways. This book uses several pathways that connect with various learning styles. Those pathways are: words, music and sounds, drawings, analyzing, body movement, nature, communication, and introspection.

To integrate those pathways with reading skills, the learning activities in this book get your students moving, making something, listening, exploring, writing, building, debating, making sounds, telling jokes, designing, acting, dancing, thinking, observing, painting, reflecting, creating, solving, playing games, interviewing, helping their communities, and more! View this book as a mini liberal arts education for your students! All of these activities have one goal: to teach key reading skills in a nonthreatening, alternative, fun way.

Every day you teach will bring new revelations about the individual personalities in your classroom. This book will help you take advantage of the innate abilities of your students, ranging from their analytical skills to their artistic ones. The projects are challenging, individualized, and definitely experiential. Talk to your students about how they like to learn. See which types of activities they gravitate toward. If students are attracted to projects that focus on sounds and drawing, you can make an educated guess about their preferred learning style. Take your cues from your students!

## Traditional Skills, Nontraditional Instruction

Use this book to teach reading skills to the whole child. The book can broaden the way your students learn and the way you teach them. Let the activities in this book unlock how your students' minds and spirits tick. Get your students out of their seats and encourage them to use their whole selves to think and learn. The reading skills covered in this book are traditional, but the methods most definitely are not!

The Eight Intelligences

Verbal-Linguistic Intelligence

Logical-Mathematical Intelligence

Bodily-Kinesthetic Intelligence

Visual-Spatial Intelligence

Musical Intelligence

Interpersonal Intelligence

Intrapersonal Intelligence

Naturalist Intelligence

0-7682-3125-6 *Creative Reading*

Verbal–Linguistic Intelligence

Logical–Mathematical Intelligence

Bodily–Kinesthetic Intelligence

Visual–Spatial Intelligence

Musical Intelligence

Interpersonal Intelligence

Intrapersonal Intelligence

Naturalist Intelligence

# Introduction

Most people comprehend better when topics are broken down into bite-size pieces, and our students are no exception. Remember, your students have only been reading for a handful of years. They need time to wrap their minds around many, many concepts. The chart below shows the core reading skills covered in the book as well as a simple way of presenting that skill to your students. This book will help you help your students think in terms of *DO*, instead of *DON'T*!

| Main Ideas and Details | Prediction | Inference | Summarization | Sequence |
|---|---|---|---|---|
| What's going on here? | Can you tell what will happen? | Clues offer conclusions! | What happened? Sum it up! | In what order did things happen? |

| Compare and Contrast | Cause and Effect | Fact and Opinion | Author's Purpose | Story Elements |
|---|---|---|---|---|
| Compare things that are the same. Contrast their differences. | Why something happened; What happened next? | Can you prove it? Or is it something that's felt or thought? | What does the author mean? | Start simple: people, plot, place, time, point of view. |

### Connections Across Concepts

Sometimes, students think in a vacuum and tend to isolate concepts. They may feel that the only times they need to use their reading skills are when they are reading or writing. Activities in this *UnWorkbook* will help them relate reading skills to many other settings and life situations. For instance, show your students that main ideas are just as important to a piece of writing as they are to an architect's blueprint or an artist's painting. Or, illustrate how cause and effect is embedded in the worlds of sports and nature.

0-7682-3125-6 *Creative Reading*

# Introduction

Use the activities in this book as you begin a new lesson or as supplemental material. Students may do the activities alone, with partners, as a whole class, or as groups within the class. Use the *UnWorkbook* to foster a collaborative effort in your classroom and to spur your students to work independently.

Some of the activities are ongoing, and one language arts session won't be nearly enough time! See where the ideas in this book take you! Perhaps you and your students will piggyback other ideas off the ones that are presented here. Some students might have a hard time with concepts that allow them so much leeway! They might be so intent on getting the "right" answers that they freeze up and can't let their imaginations work. Guide your students so they understand the key reading skills, but allow them the freedom and flexibility to execute the activities. Let them see that learning is a process.

## Think Locally

Some of the activities in this book make students think about getting involved in their local community. As a teacher, you can encourage and support the ideas of your students. Remind them that adult supervision is required for all volunteering activities.

Explain to your students that no one is too young to make a difference. Even small hands help make contributions. Let your students know how volunteering can make them feel. Allow students to clean up the school campus or care for any class pets. Give examples of your helpful contributions, too. This is a great way to lead by example, and it shows students another dimension to your personality. It's always a revelation when students see their teachers as "regular people."

Volunteering is a good way for your students to use their best skills. A great singer can volunteer for a talent show that raises money for disaster relief victims. A struggling student can see his artistic ability shine through posters for food pantry donations. A responsible student with good organizational skills would be an asset to anyone!

The aim of this book is to help all students learn and capitalize on their strengths. All students will feel better about themselves if they know they have something to offer. Helping others is a great start.

Verbal-Linguistic Intelligence

Logical-Mathematical Intelligence

Bodily-Kinesthetic Intelligence

Visual-Spatial Intelligence

Musical Intelligence

Interpersonal Intelligence

Intrapersonal Intelligence

Naturalist Intelligence

# A Film for Fifth

**Materials:** paper, pens or pencils, various props, video camera

Understanding the concept of a main idea and supporting details is crucial to a student's language arts education. However, understanding main ideas goes beyond language arts. Get your students to see that themes exist in subjects from politics to art and from business to television shows. Themes are everywhere.

Your class will work together on this ongoing project. Your job will be to guide them and offer assistance. However, let your class learn the valuable lessons of working together, organizing themselves, and compromising.

## Directions:

1. Tell your students they will be making a movie based on one aspect of being a fifth grader. That one aspect will be the main idea or theme of this movie. For instance, let's say your students complain about the hard work they must endure as fifth graders. "Hard work" is the main idea and can fit nicely into a comedy. Or, let's say your class chooses to revolve the theme around social life. One aspect of social life at this age is exclusion and gossiping. This main idea could easily be adapted to a drama, as students act out the negative effects of spreading rumors.
   The core concept you must convey to your students is that their movie must contain a clear-cut, concise main idea supported by rich and full details.

2. Ask for main idea suggestions and write them down on the board. Have the students vote for the main idea they like the most. Explain to your students that in voting for the theme, they should also consider which topic would best lend itself to making a movie.

3. After the students choose the main idea, divide them into groups. You will need three groups: one group to write the movie, one group of actors, and one group to be in charge of props, sets, and making movie posters. Let your students gravitate to the groups where they feel the most comfortable and confident. All of the students work together to decide on the title.

One language arts session is not enough time for this activity! Realize that part of the learning your students will glean from this project will be to watch the process evolve. Your job will be to film the movie when it's all done!

0-7682-3125-6 *Creative Reading*

# Wish You Were Here!

**Materials:** travel magazines, online research, or library books, pen or pencil, paper, markers or colored pencils

## Directions:

1. Browse through travel magazines, online sites, or books to give you background information on vacation spots. Jot down any information with specific details that seem interesting to you. Now think of an imaginary place you'd like to be.

2. Look at the notes you took, but don't start writing yet! Since you're dreaming up this place from your imagination, you will use your notes in a different way! Let's say you saw some pictures of the Alps and some photographs of the gorgeous beaches in South Africa. That might inspire you to have an ocean sitting on a sandy mountaintop at your location. You decide what's so incredible about your spot!

3. Write a poem about your wonderland. Describe what makes it so unique. Use details to help express your main idea. Make your language rich and exciting! Only you know why this place is so extraordinary. Let the magic of your poem entice someone to visit.

4. Use your poem to create a travel brochure with pictures and comments about this place. Then, recite your poem to your family and friends and show them your brochure. Do they want to take a trip?

_____

_____

_____

_____

_____

_____

_____

_____

_____

_____

_____

**Name** _____     **Date** _____

# It's Worth It!

**Materials:** partners, newspapers, pad for note taking, pens or pencils

**Directions:** Ask several friends to help you with this exercise. The more, the merrier! You also need your teacher or another adult to supervise you. This activity will use your talents to lend a hand to a worthy cause, and that will make anyone feel good!

1. With your partners, think of someone or something in your town that needs help. Read your local newspapers for ideas. Use the questions below to jump-start your thinking.
   - What group of people or what organization could use your help?
   - What problem could you help solve?
   - What service(s) could you offer?

     **Examples:**
       - Does your local food pantry need cereals and canned goods?
       - Does your animal shelter need money to care for the animals?
       - Could your library use more books?

2. Once you decide who to help, let them know. Have an adult assist you in contacting the organization to let them know how you plan to help. Be sure you are clear on any procedures the organization expects you to follow.

3. Get yourself organized. Decide on the best way to put your plan into action.
   - If your goal is to raise money, how will you accomplish that?
   - If you're contributing your time, how will you do that?
   - Do you need others to help? How will you let them know?
   - Should you put flyers around town? Should you put up posters in school?

4. Pay extra attention to every detail needed to achieve your goal. Make charts and lists of tasks you want to complete so that you stay organized.

5. Put your plan into action and enjoy the results! You'll find out that it's a lot of fun to make a difference!

0-7682-3125-6 *Creative Reading*

# RRRK!

**Materials:** notebook journal, pen or pencil, tape recorder

**Directions:** Before you read the story below, imagine that you are hiding in a rain forest. It's humid and steamy. You feel the mystery and enchantment of this special place. You are alone with the millions of animals who live here. Suddenly, you hear a weird commotion, and you wonder what it is. As you read this passage, think about its main idea. What is the most important aspect of the story? Watch for details that help explain the main idea and make it come alive.

The hot air hangs heavy in the sticky rain forest of the Central American nation of Belize. A boisterous **RRRK! RRRK! RRRK!** cracks the humid air. This rough, croaking racket sounds as if it's coming from a band of frogs, but this loud noise is the chattering call of the keel-billed toucan.

This blue-legged animal is the national bird of tiny Belize. It is not very good at flying and prefers hopping. Toucans don't like being alone, so they tend to live together. Brilliant yellow, red, orange, green, and black splash across the toucan's beak. While these colors are striking, the beak's size is even more amazing. It measures around seven inches long. The toucan stands about twenty inches tall. The toucan's huge mouth equals 30 percent of its height! That means if you were fifty-four inches tall, your lips would stick out about eighteen inches!

The toucan's feet are another interesting body part. They are *zygodactyl* feet. Each foot has four toes. Two toes face backward, and two toes face forward. Woodpeckers also have the same kind of feet. The toucan loves to eat fruit and gulps its food whole instead of chewing it. Guess that big beak comes in handy!

In a journal, write how you would feel if you lived in a rain forest. Then, rewrite your journal account as if you were a keel-billed toucan. Now, go outside. Shut out everything else, and do some bird watching for a half an hour. Watch only birds! You'll find that even tiny sparrows have interesting lives! Use a tape recorder to record the birds' sounds. Do you hear **RRRK**? Record your bird watching observations in your journal.

0-7682-3125-6 *Creative Reading*

# This Is What I Mean

**Materials:** paint brushes, paints (water color, acrylic, or finger paints), drawing paper

**Directions:** Sometimes, artists create abstract paintings to show their emotions. Joy might be a few big, bold pink strokes. Anger might be thick, black strokes smeared across a canvas. Often, people argue about what an abstract painting means. For this activity, you will use a passage from one of your favorite books to create a painting.

1. Choose a passage from a favorite book or short story. You might want to look for a passage that conveys a lot of feelings.

2. Pay attention to what is happening in the text as you read. What are the characters experiencing? Have you ever gone through something similar?

3. What is the primary emotion you get from reading the passage? Take a minute to write down several words that describe the feelings you get after reading.

4. Create your own abstract work of art. Take the emotions you listed in step 3 and think about what they would look like on paper. Use the space below to make a simple sketch for a painting. Translate it onto drawing paper with brush strokes or finger paints. Remember, true artists create for themselves, not others!

**Emotion(s):** _____

# Make It Wright!

**Materials:** index card, pen or pencil, plastic building blocks, blocks, modeling dough (recipe on page 96), sand, grass, sandpaper, bark, or anything else you need to construct a model of a house and its surroundings

**Directions:** Frank Lloyd Wright was a genius. Even though he died many years ago, Mr. Wright is still considered by many to be the world's greatest architect. Mr. Wright loved nature and showed his connection to it in his buildings. One of the most beautiful is Taliesin West in the Arizona desert. This former home and winter camp is flooded with light. The view of the desert and mountains from inside is awesome. The stone and wood building is part of the environment. And that's how Mr. Wright wanted it. To him, a building should blend into its natural surroundings. It should look and feel part of the landscape.

1.  Your task is to construct a house that will blend into its environment. Think about where you want your house. Do you love the beach? the mountains? the city?

2.  Once you determine your environment, design your home so it will feel and look as if it is part of its landscape. In real life, your building materials might be stone, wood, brick, or other natural elements, but for now, you'll have to make do by using plastic building blocks and modeling dough to create a model!

3.  In the space below, describe the real materials you'd use if you were transforming your model into a "real" house. Explain how your house reflects Wright's ideas.

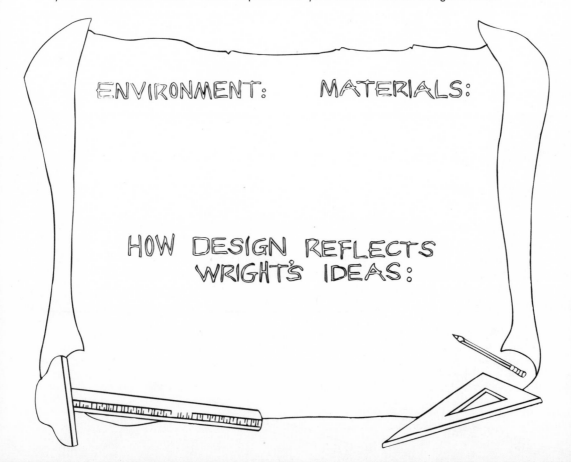

ENVIRONMENT:        MATERIALS:

HOW DESIGN REFLECTS
WRIGHT'S IDEAS:

# All About Me

**Materials:** musical instrument (optional), tape recorder, paper, pencil

**Directions:** Does your favorite television show have a theme song? Do you leave the movies humming the title tune? Do you find yourself singing a song from a commercial? Songs have a way of sticking in our heads. You might buy something because the song in the commercial convinced you that you needed it. Every song has a main idea, or theme, just like fiction and nonfiction pieces.

1. Your task is to write a theme song about yourself. Use the lyrics (words) to let people know all about YOU!

2. Pick one theme about yourself and use that as the main idea. Support this theme with lots of details. For example, if you want to show that you are a great ice skater, write lyrics that describe what you can do on the ice. Write about how you look on the ice and all about your accomplishments. What's that? You say ice skating isn't your thing? Maybe you're a great writer, a soccer star, or math wizard. Whatever it is, describe it in song . . . it doesn't have to be long!

3. If you can read music, make up your own tune on any instrument you want. If you don't read music, use the tune to a song you already know. Tape your song or play it in front of a live audience. Maybe your audience members will leave humming a tune all about you!

**All About Me**

Theme:

Details:

Lyrics:

0-7682-3125-6 *Creative Reading*

# Folks Tell

**Materials:** book of folk tales, tape recorder, oatmeal container or anything that can be used as a small drum, maraca, tambourine, or other percussion instrument

Directions: Ask fifth graders, "What is your favorite folk tale?" and you'll probably hear as many different titles as you have students. From "Paul Bunyan" and "Anansi the Spider" to "Ali Baba" and "Baba Yaga," folk tales have been a literary mainstay for hundreds and hundreds of years.

1. Explore the splendor of folk tales by reading many different versions with your students. Ask your students to identify the main ideas and details in these stories. Explain that folk tales originally were oral legends handed down from generation to generation. The legends were rich threads woven into the fabrics of those societies.

2. Your class should decide on a theme for its own folk tale. This activity will work best as a group project. If you feel your class is too large, divide it in half and do two folk tales. Have your students collaborate and agree on a main idea for their folk tale.

3. Explain that each student will contribute one or two sentences to the entire folk tale. Discuss the different ways your students can best get their theme across. Include how they can add details that will support the main idea. The students will have to think how they can move the plot along so that the last person will say the ending of the story. Logical thinking will go hand in hand with creativity for this activity.

4. Arrange your students in a circle and tape-record them. One person will begin by reciting a sentence or two. The next person will contribute one or two sentences and so on until the last person has put an ending on the tale. When the narration is complete, play it back for your class. Are the students happy with it? Does the story illustrate the main idea? Do the students want to edit and record certain parts over again?

5. When the class is satisfied with the final version, play it back. This time, let the students pantomime their own lines while the recorder plays. Or, have the students take turns acting out the tale and using percussion instruments to accompany the rhythm.

6. To expand this activity, ask other teachers if you may present your students' folk tale in their classrooms or at an assembly. In a way, your students will be acting like generations before them by repeating their folk tale orally.

**Name** _____  **Date** _____

# Will It Grow?

**Materials:** flowers or plant seeds, watering can or bottle, sunny spot, flower pot, pebbles, soil

**Directions:** A gardener watches something grow from a miniature seed into a beautiful flower or vegetable. Some people believe that gardening is the best hobby. It is relaxing, satisfying, and amazing.

1. Try gardening for yourself. Place some pebbles in the bottom of the flower pot. Fill the pot three-quarters full of soil. Push the seed(s) into the soil. Remember to cover the seeds with soil. Give your plant plenty of water and sunlight. Observe your plant every day. Some people say plants grow more if they hear human voices. Talk or sing to your plant. It might look a little odd, but it's possible that your plant will do better!

2. Make a few predictions about your plant. When will you see the first sprout? How big will your plant grow? Once your plant starts growing, see how tall it gets in one week. Will it grow the same amount every week? Forecast how much you think it will grow in one month. Can you calculate when the first bud will pop up? When will the first flower appear? Write your predictions below. Then, wait patiently to see if you were correct. Happy gardening!

| I Predict | What Really Happened | Was I Right? |
|---|---|---|
|  |  |  |
|  |  |  |
|  |  |  |
|  |  |  |
|  |  |  |
|  |  |  |

0-7682-3125-6 _Creative Reading_

# What's Next?

**Materials:** drawing paper, markers, colored pencils, or paint brushes, water colors, acrylic paints

**Directions:** Read the passage below. Can you predict what will happen?

> The class was unruly while Mrs. Beach was outside in the hall talking to Mrs. Whitaker. Erasers hurled through the air. Papers became airplanes and flew over desks. Candy bars were unwrapped and passed around. Some students danced a jig, right in the middle of the classroom. Others walked around, trying to balance books on their heads. It's unfortunate, but somehow every student, even the ones who normally never do anything wrong, participated in the rowdy behavior. One of the more adventurous students started singing in a loud voice and others joined in. That's when Mrs. Beach walked back into the room.

What happened next? Sketch your prediction in the space below. Transfer your completed design onto drawing paper. If you want, use a cartoon strip to show what happened. Your class would never act like that. Right?

0-7682-3125-6 *Creative Reading*

# It's a Mystery to Me

**Materials:** collection of short mysteries, large pieces of poster board, markers or colored pencils, drawing paper

**Directions:** There's nothing like curling up with a good mystery book. Figuring out "who done it" is one of life's small yet rewarding challenges.

1. Take advantage of the natural curiosity of your students by exposing them to some simple mysteries. Many of your students will jump at the chance to be amateur detectives and puzzle solvers. Mysteries draw students in with their settings, characters, and plot. However, a captivating mystery is one that will keep readers guessing and wanting to predict what will happen. If a mystery is too difficult or too easy to solve, students lose interest.

2. Read a short mystery that no one in the class has read before. Remind the students to pay close attention to hints and details, especially as you are reading the story aloud. Read until you feel you have reached the part where, if you read any more, you will give the mystery away. At this point, the students take over. Divide them into small groups, with six students as the maximum. Separately, each group will discuss and predict its own outcome.

3. Give each group a large piece of poster board. Tell the students to write and illustrate their predictions, but don't let them simply say, "The butler did it." If the butler did it, the students must depict *how* and *why* he did it. It will be easier for the students to divide the poster board into sections, with each section representing one page. This will force them into visualizing the ending and nudge them into thinking in a logical manner. After all, mysteries are logical puzzle pieces that fit together.

4. When the poster boards are finished, display them and have a group discussion about the predictions. Then, read the real ending of the mystery. How close or far off were the young detectives?

0-7682-3125-6 *Creative Reading*

# Your Move

**Materials:** partner, chess or checkers set, notepad and pencil

**Directions:** A good board game can exercise your brain just as much as sports can exercise your body! The more often you play, the better you will get at thinking one, two, three, or even four moves ahead of your opponent. For this activity, you will exercise your brain not only by playing but also by predicting who will win!

1. Get a partner and play seven games of chess or checkers. You don't have to play all the games at once. Use tally marks to record the number of games played and who won the games.

2. Based on the winner of these seven games, can you predict who will win the most games in the next round? Why or why not? Use the questions below to prompt your thinking.
   - Do you have enough information?
   - Have any clues offered you any conclusions?
   - Is one person a stronger player than the other?
   - Has one person played longer or more often than the other?
   - Do you think winning these games is plain luck or is strategy involved?

3. Write down your predictions about who will win the most games in the next round.

4. When you and your partner have a chance, play seven more games. Who won the most games? Were your predictions right? Why do you think they were right or wrong? Always remember to be a good sport!

**Name** _____

**Date** _____

# Pine Cones, Sunflowers, and Infinity!

**Materials:** partners, math manipulatives, construction paper, glue, scissors, drawing paper, markers or colored pencils

**Directions:** Look closely at the skin on a snake or the way the veins of a leaf branch out. Study a honeycomb or a snowflake. No matter where you look or what season it is, Mother Nature puts on a show with patterns.

Patterns have fascinated people forever. One of the most famous patterns is Fibonacci numbers. More than seven hundred years ago, an Italian math whiz named Leonardo Fibonacci entered a contest in his hometown of Pisa. Leonardo figured out this pattern: **1, 1, 2, 3, 5, 8, 13, 21, 34, 55, 89** . . . and so on until infinity! If you want to see Leonardo's pattern at its best, look at the tightly packed seeds of a sunflower. Or, check out the petals on a daisy or the segments of a pine cone.

1. Can you unlock the secret to the Fibonacci pattern?

2. Once you've mastered the Fibonacci pattern, design your own patterns. You may use math manipulatives or shapes cut from construction paper. If you want, you may draw your pattern on paper.

3. Stay away from simple ABABAB patterns. Make your patterns challenging! And remember this: "Once is an instance, twice may be an accident, but three or more times makes a pattern!" Your design must repeat three times before it is considered a pattern.

4. See if your partners can figure out your patterns. Can they predict what comes next in the series? Can you predict what comes next in your partners' patterns?

5. Have fun making your partners crazy!

Published by Frank Schaffer Publications. Copyright protected.

0-7682-3125-6 _Creative Reading_

# Can You Tell a Joke?

**Materials:** partners, pen or pencil, index cards

**Directions:** To many people, e.e. cummings was a brilliant American poet, but he was also an intelligent man who saw the need for humor in our everyday lives. In fact, he once said, "The most wasted of all days is one without laughter." What else could you expect from a man who never wrote with capital letters? For this activity, keep in mind mr. cummings' wonderful thought!

1. Divide your students into two teams. Each team will get a chance to be kings and queens of comedy by making up jokes. To make this extra challenging, all jokes must be on one topic.

2. Team A starts by creating six jokes, all in question-and-answer form. The jokes should be short, simple, and written as a team. The question part of each joke should be on one index card, the answer (or punch line) should be on a second index card.

3. When the joke writing is finished, place all the index cards face up on the floor.

4. To play: Team B must spread out and look at all of the cards on the floor. Their job is to decide which punch lines go with which questions. Tell the students to look carefully at the choices. Since the jokes are on the same subject, some punch lines could appear to match more than one question. Team B should ask, "Is this punch line a humorous yet logical answer to the joke's question?"

5. When Team B has matched up its questions and punch lines, Team A will let them know how good (or bad!) their forecasting skills were. Then, it's Team B's turn to be the joke writers and Team A's turn to forecast the punch lines.

0-7682-3125-6 *Creative Reading*

**Name** _____    **Date** _____

# Working Backwards

**Materials:** partners, pen or pencil

**Directions:** The paragraphs below are the middle and ending paragraphs to a newspaper article. Instead of reading a passage and trying to predict what will happen next, you need to predict what happened *first*. Reverse your thinking!

> The Sleepy River School became a shelter. Nearly one hundred people needed a place to stay. The wind had blown the roofs off of some houses. Other houses were full of water—the Sleepy River wasn't so sleepy. It was three feet higher than normal! Electricity in half of the town was out. Trees were down and so were some electrical wires. School was postponed until the end of the week.
>
> Mother Nature definitely wreaked some havoc here. Thankfully, no one was hurt. And it wasn't as bad as what had been predicted. Everyone agreed with the mayor that, "Buildings are replaceable."

Once you predict what happened first, write a beginning paragraph. This will set the scene for the two paragraphs above that the author already wrote. Your partners will write their own beginning paragraphs too. Then, act out each story, using the opening paragraphs that each of you imagined. Did you and your partners have beginnings that were the same or different? Whose made the most sense? Why?

**What Happened FIRST?**

_____

_____

_____

_____

_____

_____

_____

_____

_____

_____

_____

0-7682-3125-6 *Creative Reading*

# Weather or Not!

**Materials:** pen or pencil, possible: pan to catch rainfall, ruler to measure snowfall

**Directions:** Use this weather chart every day for ten days. Does the temperature rise or fall? Remember to measure the amount of snow or rain you receive. At the end of the ten days, examine your chart. Can you tell anything from the temperatures? Were there mostly sunny, rainy, or cloudy days? Use your data to predict the weather for the following five days. After you make your forecast, chart the weather for the next five days. How accurate were your predictions?

**Ten-Day Weather Record:**

| Date | Temperature | Weather | Comments |
|---|---|---|---|
|  |  |  |  |
|  |  |  |  |
|  |  |  |  |
|  |  |  |  |
|  |  |  |  |
|  |  |  |  |
|  |  |  |  |
|  |  |  |  |
|  |  |  |  |
|  |  |  |  |

**I Predict:**

Avg. Temp: _____    No. of Snowy Days: _____    No. of Sunny Days: _____

Avg. Weekly Snowfall: _____    No. of Cloudy Days: _____    No. of Rainy Days: _____

Avg. Weekly Rainfall: _____

**What Really Happened:**

| Date | Temperature | Weather | Comments |
|---|---|---|---|
|  |  |  |  |
|  |  |  |  |
|  |  |  |  |
|  |  |  |  |
|  |  |  |  |

# Rise or Fall?

**Materials:** financial pages with stock market quotes, pens or pencils

**Directions:** Anybody can predict. Weathermen do it all the time. Pollsters forecast who will win political races. Those who play the stock market bet that the prices of their stocks will rise.

1. Give your students a crash course on the stock market. Keep it simple! Explain the basics: Shareholders own a piece of a company. When the company does well, the price of its stock rises. If shareholders sell at that point, they make money. If the company doesn't do well, the price of its stock declines. If shareholders sell at that point, they lose money.

2. You should arbitrarily choose ten companies in which the students could "invest." Then, divide your class into groups, with six students as the maximum. Each group must pick one of the ten companies you selected. The groups cannot pick the same companies. If a conflict arises, use a lottery system to solve it.

3. Have your students examine the stock prices of their companies in the newspaper. Show them the highs and lows. Let the class study the prices for two weeks. Do the students detect any trends with their stock prices? Are they increasing, decreasing, or staying the same?

4. Tell your students that based on their research they must make some predictions about where the prices of their stocks will be one month from now. Each group must forecast whether its company's stock will rise, fall, or stay the same. If the students feel the stock prices will rise or fall, have them forecast the ending prices. Explain to your students that the prices they see in the paper are influencing their predictions. In reality, analysts look at a myriad of factors that will affect a stock price.

5. Create a chart similar to the one below for students to record their predictions. There are no winners or losers here, just plain fun to see if fifth graders can outwit the stock market!

| Stock Name | Original Price | Predict Price Will Go To | Actual Price at the End of One Month |
|---|---|---|---|
|  |  |  |  |
|  |  |  |  |
|  |  |  |  |
|  |  |  |  |

0-7682-3125-6 *Creative Reading*

# One Look

**Materials:** index cards, pens or pencils

**Directions:** Without your even speaking to them, your students can infer from one look on your face that it's time for them to get serious about working. Your students notice the clues given by your facial expressions and mannerisms. Inferencing is an important reading skill, but it is also a handy "people" skill to know. At this age, interpreting social clues and facial expressions are very important to a student's social life.

1.  Divide your students into small groups, with six students as the maximum. Have each group write a description of two social scenes on index cards. For example, they might portray a scenario about three friends enjoying a sleepover or several students excluding another from a game. They could write about a family problem or a family triumph. Or, they could write about something that happened at lunchtime. Five or six succinct lines should depict each situation.

2.  Have the students take turns acting out their scenarios in pantomime. See if the other students can infer what is happening by the actions, body language, social clues, and facial expressions of the actors. Explain to your students that the combination of these small pieces of evidence allows their classmates to arrive at conclusions about the big picture.

3.  Can the students infer what has happened in the scenarios? Can they guess the big picture? After all, understanding the big picture isn't just important for reading proficiency. It's important for everyday life!

**Name**                             **Date**

# This Is What I Think

**Materials:** partner, whistling skills, empty oatmeal container or small drum, musical instruments (optional)

**Directions:** Read the scene below. It tells you that something happened. Yet, it doesn't tell you exactly *what* happened. You will work with a partner to piece the details together based on the evidence.

> The back door was ajar. Muddy footprints tracked everywhere. The smell of oatmeal raisin cookies hung in the air. A plate, shattered into a million pieces, lay scattered on the tiled floor. A few remaining cookies were spread out on the table. My mother walked into the kitchen and took one look at me. I knew I had to explain.

1.  Can you tell from the clues what happened here? This story could go in several directions. It all depends on how you interpret the scene. Discuss with your partner what you each think might have happened. Then agree on one conclusion that makes the most sense.

2.  With your partner, write a song based on what you think happened. If you can read music, make up your own tune on any instrument you want. If you don't read music, use the tune to a song you already know. One partner should sing the song while the other one whistles the tune or beats out the rhythm on the drum. Think about how the music can set the mood for the action. For example, the music can build to a climax (most dramatic part) for the most exciting action.

3.  Once you have practiced, you can perform your song for the rest of the class. How does your interpretation of what happened differ from what others thought? How is it the same? How does the music reflect what is happening in the action?

     0-7682-3125-6 *Creative Reading*

# Look Closely

**Materials:** art book, drawing paper, paint brushes, acrylic paints or watercolors

**Directions:** Ask your teacher for an art book or borrow one from the library. Look at the pictures carefully. Choose one that you like. Use the picture to answer the questions below.

1. Look closely at the details in your picture. Draw some conclusions about the picture based on the details you see. **Example:** A picture of a baby walking towards its parents is simple to figure out. Or is it? Look closely at the parents and the baby. Are the parents unusually excited? Is the baby teetering and tottering? These details and clues tell you that these are the baby's first steps. Use the questions below to help you draw conclusions.

   - What is the main focus of the picture you chose? Is it a scene, a person, an event?
   - Does your picture have a title? If so, what clues does the title give you about what is happening in the scene?
   - What do the colors and style of the picture tell you about the mood?

   Based on details, I think

   _____

   _____

2. Can you relate any feelings of your own to the feelings or tone of the picture you chose? Use a day in your life and draw a picture that reflects the same mood portrayed in the picture you selected. Make sure your details help an admirer draw some conclusions. Think about how you could use color to set a certain mood. Use the space below to make a beginning sketch of your idea.

**Name** _____          **Date** _____

# Actions Speak Louder Than Words

**Materials:** partners, index cards, pencils, small containers or baskets, timer, chalkboard and chalk or sheet of paper and marker to keep score

**Directions:** Divide into teams. Each person should get at least two index cards. Write down one noun on each card. Make your words interesting and don't show them to your teammates! Each team should put index cards in its own container. Mark the containers _Team A_, _Team B_, and so on.

**To play:**

1. Start with Team A. One person at a time must pull one index card from the container. If you pick one of the words you made up, try again.

2. Once you have your noun, you must portray that word to your own teammates through actions. You may use sounds, but no talking! Here's an example: If you must depict "tea kettle," you could move your body so you look like an object that is pouring something. Whistling could tip off your teammates that you are a "tea kettle." The object is to do whatever you can so that your teammates will draw the right conclusions based on your actions. Don't be afraid to use your body to get the word across! If you get the word _pretzel_, good luck with that one!

3. You will have two minutes to guess the answer. Use a timer to signal the end of time. The team that makes the most right guesses wins.

0-7682-3125-6 _Creative Reading_

# Hidden Meanings

**Materials:** pens or pencils, paper

**Directions:** Everywhere we look, we interpret symbols as words. A smiley face signifies happiness, and a forefinger wrapped in string is a reminder. A knife and fork on a highway sign means a restaurant is nearby, and a figure in a wheelchair signifies handicapped accessibility. An eight-sided polygon, even with the word *STOP* omitted, will still make most drivers press the brake pedal.

All of these symbols allow us to infer meanings. Inference is an integral part of reading comprehension. A student who can master inferencing will do well comprehending the big picture and the nuances of a written piece. This activity will sharpen your students' inferencing skills by having them look at symbols in written text.

1. Divide your class into small groups, with six students as the maximum. Each group is responsible for creating a short story that combines symbols with written words. Your students should insert the symbols into appropriate places in their short stories. The symbols may be well known, or the students may make up their own symbols.

2. Explain that all symbols must represent a single word or phrase. The reader must be able to infer the symbols' meanings from sentence context clues.

   Example: "This ⌂ , I had to be quiet. No one was up yet."

   The symbol ⌂ represents morning. At first, the reader may think it means *sun* or even *sunset*. But the context clues ("I had to be quiet. No one was up yet") let the reader infer that the writer means *morning*.

3. Tell the groups they must use at least one symbol in every sentence.

4. When the stories are finished, have the students exchange them with each other. See if the students can understand the stories' meanings and infer what is going on from the symbols and the written words of their classmates.

5. When all the stories are written, have the students act out their stories.

0-7682-3125-6 *Creative Reading*

**Name** _____     **Date** _____

# ♫ Can You Hear It?

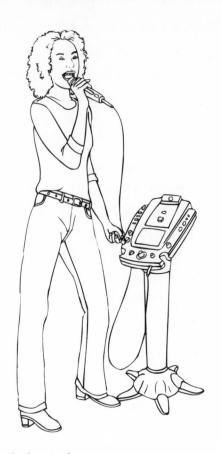

## Directions:

1. For this activity, relax and listen to a few songs that don't have any lyrics. Classical music, jazz pieces, and instrumentals will work perfectly. Write the title(s) of the songs you chose in the chart below.

2. As you listen, write down how you think the artists felt as they created this music. The tone and sound of the music will give you some clues. The instruments used for the songs will also hint at their moods. Record your thoughts in the chart below.

3. Now, show the mood you're in today. Make your own music by humming or whistling a tune, adding some drum beats, strums from a guitar, or shakes from a tambourine. Even a playful laugh or a humorous, "YAHOO!" will help. The sounds you use will let a listener infer what you're feeling. If you play a musical instrument, compose a new song that will reveal today's emotions.

4. Record your song or play it for someone else. See if a friend can guess your mood from the song you made. Maybe someday, your song will rise to number one on the charts!

| Song Title | Mood Expressed in the Song |
|---|---|
|  |  |
|  |  |
|  |  |
|  |  |

0-7682-3125-6 _Creative Reading_

# Can You Guess?

**Materials:** pen or pencil, tape recorder (optional)

**Directions:** Read the sentences below. Each sentence is a clue about the theme of this page.

- I have something in common with the continents.
- ROYGBIV and the colors of the rainbow also give you a clue.
- If you take away my first letter, you get a kind of number.
- If you squeeze a "T" between my first and second letters, you will spell a boy's name.
- I have something in common with the days of the week, especially Tuesday.
- I'm a pal to the number 49.

I am _____ _____ _____ _____ _____.

After you've guessed what I am, write a four-line poem about me. Record it and set it to music if you want.

_____

_____

_____

_____

Published by Frank Schaffer Publications. Copyright protected.

0-7682-3125-6 *Creative Reading*

# Match 'Em Up!

**Materials:** partners, index cards, pens or pencils

**Directions:** How do your students view themselves? This game will give you some insight into your students, and it will let them use their detective skills along the way.

1. First, the students must write down two of their best or worst qualities on "Q" cards. After the students do this, have them jot down examples of something they've done to illustrate each quality. These will be the "E" cards. For instance, if a student writes down *patient* on a Q card, the matching E card could be, "I stood in line for three hours at Disney World and never complained." The cards shouldn't have any names on them.

2. To play: Divide your students equally into a Q and an E team. Put the Q cards in one pile, the E cards in another and shuffle them. Each Q team player chooses a quality card. Each E team player picks an example card. If students select their own cards, have them try again.

3. The first Q team member will recite the quality he or she chose. E team players must discuss whose example (if any) matches the Q card quality. Let's say that the E team is confident one member has a match. That E team player must surrender the matching card to you. In addition, the Q team player must surrender the Q card to you. Keep all matches together. The players who made the matches draw cards to replace the ones they surrendered.

4. If, however, the E team feels there isn't a match for a particular Q card, both the E and Q players hold onto their cards until their next turns. Their matches may show up in subsequent rounds. The next Q player displays his or her quality, and the E team must try to find a match. The students play out this sequence until each Q card has an appropriate mate.

5. The previous paragraph pointed out that "their matches *may* show up in subsequent rounds." The word *may* is used because the students may be erroneously pairing up the cards earlier in the game. If this happens, succeeding cards won't have any suitable matches! Remind your students to use their detective skills and look for clues in the sentences!

6. The game is over when every card has a match, or when the students feel they can't correctly pair up the remaining cards. Read the paired cards and ask the students who wrote them if the matches are correct. If not, let the card owners correctly match them up. The class will see its mistakes. How did your private eyes do?

Published by Frank Schaffer Publications.    0-7682-3125-6 *Creative Reading*

# Eight Letters to My Name

**Materials:** survey respondents, pencil

**Directions:** Use the clues below to solve this riddle. Once you've cracked it, read the poem to your friends and family. Can they figure it out? Use the chart to record their answers. Also, mark down the clues your respondents say gave the riddle away. Does everyone point to the same clues? On a separate sheet of paper, take out the giveaway clues. Put in your own clues to make the poem even harder! Try it out on some unsuspecting detectives.

### Eight Letters to My Name

I travel to and fro and I'm often on the go

Until I have to stop, and then

I might stay at the house of Gwen or Ben or even Sven.

Sometimes, I have something inside,

I can be skinny or rather wide.

There's not much to me, but I do have a flap,

And I'm carried to places all over the map.

Be careful with me, I could cut your tongue,

But with me, you'll never get stung.

There are times when I'm returned or rejected,

And then I feel dejected.

There are eight letters in my name,

Three of them are the same.

I'm often sealed tight

With a stamp on my right.

Good luck figuring me out,

I think you'll do it, without a doubt!

| Name | Defining Clue | What Am I? |
|------|---------------|------------|
|      |               |            |
|      |               |            |
|      |               |            |
|      |               |            |

Check your answer on the Answer Key, page 96.

# Boil It Down!

**Directions:** Summarizing is truly an art. This activity will help your students learn more about summarizing through their experiences and get them up and moving to create their own on-the-spot summaries.

1. Point out to your students that summaries are a part of their everyday lives! When they watch TV, they see the features of an automobile squeezed into a thirty-second commercial. When they're at the movies, a preview or "trailer" boils down the plot of an upcoming film. When they look at a book they might buy, the jacket flap sums up the story line for them.

2. Tell your students to think on their feet for this project! Pair up your students. One student quickly tells a simple, three- or four-sentence story.

3. Just as quickly, the other student sums up the story by using a few hand gestures, body and facial movements, and sounds. Do this repeatedly and move the students around so they get new partners.

4. This activity should take place for all pairs of students at the same time. It might get a little noisy, but it will certainly be fun!

0-7682-3125-6 *Creative Reading*

# How to Make a Keel-Billed Toucan

**Materials:** markers or colored pencils

**Directions:** The words and phrases below all relate to a keel-billed toucan. Use the words to help you draw a picture of this brilliantly colored bird in the box below.

loves fruit, especially apples, bananas, mangos, cantaloupe, papayas

humongous beak is yellow, red, orange, green, and black

feet are zygodactyl, legs are blue

lives together with at least six other birds in rain forests in South and Central America

sleeps in tree holes

RRRK!

doesn't fly well

body is black with small red V-section under its tail

chest, face, and neck are yellow

area around eyes and small lines on either side of beak are green

thin red border goes around its yellow chest

0-7682-3125-6 *Creative Reading*

**Name** _____                     **Date** _____

# Think Straight!

**Materials:** thirty large paper clips, highlighter

**Directions:** If you follow these directions, you will make an alphabet letter from ten paper clips. However, you don't need all the sentences to create the paper-clip letter. Use your brain to reason this out. Highlight or underline the sentences you need. You can sum up the directions in three sentences. Read the entire paragraph at least once before you start highlighting. It's tricky, so pay attention! (Even to these directions!)

Scatter the paper clips all over the table. Be careful not to drop them on the floor. Count out twenty paper clips. Do you have a recycle center in your town? Now count out ten paper clips. Attach all the clips together. Dangle the clips from the edge of the table. Make sure you don't use hair clips instead. Three clips go across the top. Don't use small paper clips for this exercise. You should recycle paper. There's your letter! You could not make this letter with a rubber band. Four clips, from the top down, slant diagonally to the left. Cloth, fiber, and wood are paper ingredients. Can you make a paper clip out of paper? Drag the clips around the table so they make a clanking sound. Three clips go across on the bottom. Jumble the clips into a giant heap.

0-7682-3125-6 _Creative Reading_

# Film This!

**Materials:** partners, pencils, tape recorder

**Directions:** Hurray for Hollywood! Pretend that you and your partners are off to make a movie. Do you want a comedy or drama? What time span will your film cover? What will happen? All the partners have a say in this movie. The key is to cooperate and work well together.

Once you've decided what your movie will be about write a "treatment" on the lines below. That's movie talk for a summary. Sum up the plot, characters, and setting. Tape record your summary so you can send it to some Hollywood executives. If they like it, they could produce your movie! These execs don't have a lot of time. Your summary shouldn't be long. But it must state the main points of your film. Convince Hollywood that this flick is worth it!

_____

_____

_____

_____

_____

_____

# Once

**Directions:** Choose one event in your life that has special meaning to you. You will use that event to do the activity below.

1. Remember everything you can about the event you chose. Think of everything that occurred during that experience and record your notes on the lines below.

_____

_____

_____

_____

2. Now, sum the experience up in a few lines. Only use those details that will illustrate the important aspects of your experience.

_____

_____

_____

_____

3. Based on your summary, create a dance that will depict this event. Connect the mood of your event to your body movements. If it's a happy mood, you may want to jump or skip as you dance. If the mood is sad, you may want to move your body slowly. If your experience made you anxious, move your body in a halting manner. Remember to use facial expressions as you dance; they are great ways to summarize and demonstrate your feelings!

# Hot Spots

**Materials:** survey respondents, pen or pencil

**Directions:** Interview family members and friends and ask them which continent, country, or state they would like to visit. What is the main reason this place fascinates them? Use the chart below to write down their answers. Then, take one sentence that each person said and use it in a poem about "Hot Spots." Recite your poem in front of an audience!

| Place | Why Visit |
|-------|-----------|
|       |           |
|       |           |
|       |           |
|       |           |

**Hot Spots Poem**

_____

_____

_____

_____

_____

_____

_____

_____

_____

_____

**Name** _____     **Date** _____

# Give It a Swirl

**Materials:** finger paints, several sheets of drawing paper, video camera or tape recorder

**Directions:**

1.  Finger paints are a great a medium to express your feelings! Gather several different colors of finger paint and drawing paper. Use each finger paint color on a separate sheet of paper.

2.  Create at least one different design for each color. Some designs may be big and brash while others may be quiet wisps.

3.  When you are finished with your designs, examine your strokes. Under each design, write one word that sums it up. Does it look *aggressive* or *timid*? Does it look *beautiful*? Does it remind you of something *daring* or *courageous*?

4.  Now, take those one-word summaries and create a dance that will match them in feeling. Dance bold. Dance quiet. Dance thoughtful. Give your dancing shoes a workout!

5.  Let an adult videotape your dance. Before you begin each dance, explain which design you are dancing. If you don't have a video camera, use a tape recorder to explain how you performed each dance.

0-7682-3125-6 *Creative Reading*

# Circle, Square, Triangle, or . . .

**Materials:** various geometric shapes cut from construction paper, poster board, scissors, glue

**Directions:** If you were to ask your students how they spent their lunchtime, you might get spontaneous, enthusiastic, high-spirited accounts of various incidents. Ask them to sum it up in three or four sentences, and silence is what you might hear!

Sometimes, students freeze when they hear the word *summarize*. Take the mystery out of summarizing. Tell your students to close their eyes after reading a chapter in a novel. What do they remember? What images do they see in their mind's eye? What they remember and what they envision are the starting points for their summaries. Anything we read is easily turned into "What happened in the beginning? What happened in the middle? What happened at the end?" If your students learn to break apart what they read this way, summarizing will be a piece of cake!

1. For this activity, let the students choose what they want to summarize. It can range from a poem to a real-life incident.

2. The actual thinking starts once the students sum up their beginnings, middles, and ends. Each segment must be represented by geometric shapes. For instance, a tangle of triangles layered on top of each other may symbolize dilemmas faced by a protagonist in the beginning of a chapter. Smooth sequential circles could symbolize the serene middle of a poem. Two hemispheres placed on top of each other and opening up could signify a triumphant ending.

3. This activity will not be easy! However, it will help your students think logically about summarizing. Even the most dramatic, fictional piece has logic in it. Let your students have fun deciding which shapes to use and how to use them. Let them change and rearrange the shapes to portray exactly what they want.

4. When your students are satisfied with their geometric summaries, they should glue them on the poster board. When the gluing is complete, have the students present their summaries. They should be interesting!

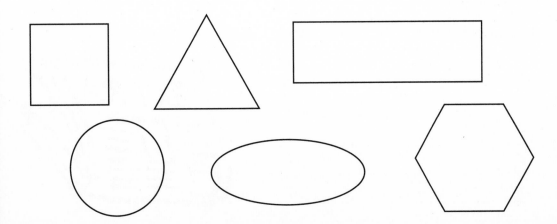

0-7682-3125-6 *Creative Reading*

**Name** _____  **Date** _____

# Dear Editor

**Materials:** pen, stationery

**Directions:** Think of a topic that is important to you. Do you wish there were more appropriate television shows for children your age? Do drivers speed through streets where you and your friends play? Are there people in your town who don't vote, even though they have that privilege? Should your town have a garden? Does everyone in your town have enough food to eat?

Choose a topic that is close to your heart and fills you with passion. Then, write a letter to the editor of your local newspaper or school paper. Briefly and clearly, summarize your point of view. State why you feel the way you do. Summarize a plan of action that will help the situation. Other people may have thought about this same topic but didn't act on it. You just might get the ball rolling!

Dear Editor,

_____

_____

_____

_____

_____

_____

_____

_____

_____

_____

_____

_____

_____

_____

_____

_____

0-7682-3125-6 *Creative Reading*

# Design Center

**Materials:** large pieces of poster board, pencils, writing and drawing paper, markers or colored pencils, tape recorder, video camera (optional)

**Directions:** Without plans, nothing in this world is accomplished. Plans are based on order and sequencing. Show your students how much of their daily patterns are organized around sequential ordering. Even getting out the door in the morning has a certain order to it.

1. Divide your class into small groups, with six students as the maximum. Each group will be responsible for designing a new product.

2. First, students must agree on which product type they want to tackle. The choices are nonelectronic toy, an automobile, nonviolent video game, a different kind of backpack, and a piece of furniture. More than one group may choose to design the same product.

3. After the groups select their products, they must write down, in order, the steps they'll need to create their designs. Explain to your class that simply sitting down and sketching out a new car isn't the proper sequence for a successful design. Each group must consider the product's purpose and what materials will be used to make it. Students must know what the product will accomplish and who will buy it. If they want to design a chair, should they design it for a kid's room, or should they design it for an older person? The response will dictate the chair's design.

4. For those students already imagining a new car on the road, explain how different their design will be if they gear the car to a young, sporty driver instead of a soccer mom. Students must also ask, "What will this product do?" Tell the class that answering questions about their products will translate into better designs. Let them see that a clear order organizes their thinking and leads them to their goals.

5. Have the students sketch out rough drafts on drawing paper. Let them know it is normal to do more than one draft—writers do that all the time! When your students are satisfied with their drafts, have them transfer them to big pieces of poster board for the final coloring. Remind students to label their designs with important information.

6. Have the students present their designs to the class. Use a tape recorder or video camera to capture the presentations. This activity might even make your students look at a chair or car in a different light! Hopefully, it will make them more aware of how crucial sequencing is, not only in reading, but in practically everything we do.

**Name** _____    **Date** _____

# Pack Up!

**Materials:** glue, scissors, pencil

**Directions:** You are going on a long journey. You will be exploring the North Pole, scuba diving in the Caribbean, and visiting museums in New York. Below are the names of some traveling items. There's also a drawing of an empty suitcase. Cut out the names of the items. Arrange them so their order matches the order of the places you will travel to first, second, and third. The first items you need will be on the right hand side of the suitcase. The last items you need will be on the bottom of the suitcase, or the left side of it. Once you've arranged the items glue them into place. Remember, your first stop is the North Pole!

| sunscreen | scarf | snow suit |
|---|---|---|
| parka | knitted hat | bathing suit |
| flip flops | nice shoes | sweaters |
| mittens | collapsible ski poles | nice dress coat |
| scuba gear | woolen socks | boots |

0-7682-3125-6 _Creative Reading_

# ROYGBIV and Me

**Materials:** paper, colored pencils that match rainbow colors, stapler, or ribbon and hole punch

**Directions:** If you're lucky, you've seen a few rainbows by now. An easy way to remember the awesome colors are: **R**ed, **O**range, **Y**ellow, **G**reen, **B**lue, **I**ndigo, and **V**iolet. **ROYGBIV!**

Colors can often trigger different emotions in us. Green is a peaceful color while red is a fiery shade. Sometimes, a color will remind us of our past.

Think of seven events in your life that are important to you.

1. Match those events to the seven colors of the rainbow. To do this, start by pairing up your events with the colors in the order the events happened. For instance, red should match an episode that happened when you were little. Does red remind you of riding your first red tricycle? Violet should match the most recent event. Does violet make you think of your first day in fifth grade? If it will help, use the chart below.

2. Now, make a book about your life. With your colored pencils, lightly shade each sheet of paper in rainbow colors. Next, illustrate these pages to show your special occasions. Leave room at the bottom of each page to write a short poem about each specific day.

3. Staple your book together or use a hole punch and thread ribbon through the holes. You are an author and illustrator!

| Red | Orange | Yellow | Green | Blue | Indigo | Violet |
|-----|--------|--------|-------|------|--------|--------|
| 1.  | 2.     | 3.     | 4.    | 5.   | 6.     | 7.     |

**Name** _____     **Date** _____

# Funny Food

**Materials:** markers or colored pencils

**Directions:** Use the boxes below to draw a cartoon strip. Draw your pictures in the order the events will happen. Don't use any dialogue in this cartoon. Rely only on your drawings to get your point across. There's only one catch—food must be your cartoon's main idea! For example, in the first square, a girl could water a small watermelon plant. The watermelon grows much bigger in the second square. By the third square, the watermelon is humongous. The fourth square contains the only solution: a bunch of kids dig into the watermelon, and everyone has a feast!

| 1. | 2. |
|---|---|
| | |
| **3.** | **4.** |
| | |

0-7682-3125-6 *Creative Reading*

# Don't Talk!

**Materials:** partners (optional), various props, cartoon strip created in "Funny Food" on page 46

**Directions:**

1. For the activity on this page, you'll need the cartoon strip you created for "Funny Food" on page 46.

2. Act out your cartoon in pantomime. In pantomime, actors don't speak. They use gestures and facial expressions to act out their stories.

3. Use partners if you need them. Remember, no talking!

4. After you've acted out the cartoon once, go back and do it again, but this time, act it out backwards.

5. Now, try this: Don't act out the fourth square the way you drew it. Take thirty seconds to devise a new ending and act it out right away! Actors call that "improvising." Break a leg! (That's stage talk for "Good luck!")

**Name** _____    **Date** _____

 # It's Easy as 1-2-3

**Materials:** pen or pencil, old clothes, various items that will help you do a chore

**Directions:**

1. Find a chore you can do that will help someone in your family. Choose a task you've never done before. Do you have the ability to do this? How long will it take? How will this help your family member?

2. Get permission to do this chore from an adult in your house. If you can do the chore, ask an adult to supervise your work.

3. Before you start, consider the most efficient way to get the job done. As you do this chore, write down each step on the first set of lines below. Step one should be how you decided on the perfect, useful task!

4. Time yourself from the start to the finish of this chore.

5. Once your mission is accomplished, analyze what you did and how you did it. You followed certain steps in a precise sequence. Think about whether you could have done your task in a different sequence. Could this new order require less time? Write the new steps on the second set of lines.

6. When you get a chance, do this chore again with your new order. Did the second sequence require less time to accomplish the same task? If your time was faster, do you think it is because of the order or because you're more experienced at the task?

_____

_____

_____

_____

_____

_____

_____

_____

_____

_____

_____

_____

_____

0-7682-3125-6 *Creative Reading*

# School Spirit!

**Materials:** paper, pen or pencil, musical instrument (optional), tape recorder

**Directions:**

1. Your school principal has chosen you to compose a new song for your school. If you can read music, make up your own tune on any instrument you want. If you can't read musical notes, use the tune to a song you already know.

2. Your principal wants the song to be six lines long. The lyrics in the first line must include the school's name.

3. The lyrics for the next line must describe the town where your school is located. What would a school be without its teachers?

4. For the third line, say something about the school's teachers. The fourth line must describe the cafeteria food. (You can say whether it's good or bad!) If there isn't a cafeteria at your school, have this line focus on lunchtime aromas.

5. The next line must say why your school is special to you.

6. And the last line can be anything you want to say about your school. If you are a homeschooled student, write a six-line song about your homeschool experiences.

7. Make your song noteworthy and record it. Would you like to play it for your principal?

**Our School Song**

_____

_____

_____

_____

_____

_____

_____

_____

_____

# Making Money

**Materials:** various items ranging from modeling dough (recipe on page 96) and construction paper to beads, paper clips, or other small items

**Directions:**

1. You and your friends have formed a new country. As of now, your country does not have a monetary system. There aren't any dollar bills, pennies, dimes, or anything else to use for currency. Your task: create money!

2. How do you do that? First, write down the steps you should follow to set up a new monetary system. Write down which denominations or values you want to use. For instance, will you want a value that equals a quarter? Do you want a coin-free society that uses only paper money? Will your paper money go as high as a one-million dollar bill? That would be a lot of change for a 75¢ candy bar!

3. Once you've settled on your money values, decide which materials you'll use to make your money. Will one bead equal a dime? Will a purple rubber band equal ten dollars? Use different materials for each different value. Be practical with your material choices. People have to walk around with this money in their pockets!

4. Will you put buildings and famous people on your money? If so, who or what will you use?

5. In the U.S., the Treasury Department ships new money to banks. The banks distribute the money to their customers. Will your new country have banks that issue money?

6. On the lines below, write down the steps you need to create a monetary system.

7. Think logically! Then, use whatever items you'd like to make samples of your money. Give them to family and friends but remind them they can't use them to pay for a milk shake!

_____

_____

_____

_____

_____

_____

_____

_____

_____

_____

       0-7682-3125-6 *Creative Reading*

# ABC or +~/

**Materials:** index cards, pencils, large pieces of butcher paper, finger paints

**Directions:** The alphabet is one of the most sequential and logically ordered systems in the world. Science tells us that the first alphabet was probably devised in 1600 B.C. in Egypt. Your students may not go down in history, but this activity will give them a chance to see sequencing at its best. Your fifth graders use sequential ordering every time they read or write. They read in a pattern, tracking from left to right, and they write the same way. Without this order, our communication system would not work. See how well your students can communicate with a new alphabet they have devised.

1. Divide your students into small groups, with six students as the maximum. Remind students to think logically, efficiently, and realistically when inventing their letters. No one wants to spend more than a second jotting down a letter. An elaborate stroke with numerous tails and serifs may look beautiful, but it won't be practical. Vertical alphabets, right to left alphabets, or any other alphabets are possible! Any new or existing symbols are acceptable. For instance, a star might be the letter B or an eye might symbolize the letter I! Your students may choose to blend sounds together. A square might say "CH," or a * could represent "TH."

2. Have the students put their new letters on index cards and then have them finger paint those letters onto poster board. Leave extra room on the paper for the students to put their new alphabet to work.

3. Below each new language system, have your students describe, in sequential order, "How to Formulate a New Alphabet." But they must use their new alphabet to write this expository piece! This won't be easy! The students should probably write this out on scrap paper first and then transfer it to the poster board.

4. *&^# ~+=! (Have fun!)

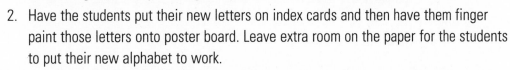

# Schoolkids

**Materials:** large chart, markers, paper, markers or colored pencils

**Directions:** It's a prerequisite of childhood that children always want to be older than they are. They constantly remind us that they are "going on 11" or "10 and a half." A school is the perfect atmosphere in which to observe all the differences among school-age children. Your fifth graders may be the oldest children in an elementary school. Or, they may be the youngest in a middle school, or the in-betweens at a K–8 school. The different grade levels will be the focus for this lesson in comparing and contrasting. If your students are homeschooled, use siblings, relatives, or family friends of different ages.

1. Compare and contrast your fifth graders with the various grade levels in your school (or siblings, relatives, friends). Write the similarities and differences on a large chart.

2. Let the categories for comparisons come from your students. They will automatically point out obvious contrasts, such as physical characteristics, and the amount of homework first graders and fifth graders receive. However, see if your students detect the finer distinctions among the ages. Do they understand that a thirteen-year-old has more freedoms and responsibilities than a ten-year-old? Can your students find comparisons with the age groups? Do all students learn certain subjects? Are there more commonalities between fifth graders and fourth graders than fifth graders and second graders?

3. This is also a good opportunity to have a discussion about growing up. Do your students perceive that older students are more independent than younger ones? Do they feel that people get more confident as they get older? Do they think that older children have more to do?

4. Expand this idea and have your students make a booklet with photographs (or illustrations) of themselves at various ages. They can compare and contrast their own lives at different ages. Which age has been the best so far? Which age are they most anxious to reach?

0-7682-3125-6 *Creative Reading*

**Compare and Contrast**

# Treasure Hunt

**Materials:** empty bag for collecting, magnifying glass, large and sturdy piece of cardboard, glue, stapler, tape, pencil and marker

**Directions:**

1. Go outside and explore. Hunt for leaves, twigs, empty wasp nests, shells, cocoons, rocks, or any other small treasures that nature has left behind. Put these items in your bag.

2. Once you've finished collecting, examine your fortune. Write down some observations on the clipboard below. Do these objects remind you of other things?

3. Glue, tape, or staple your items to the cardboard. Leave enough room under each treasure so you can write a few lines.

4. After you've attached the items, use metaphors and similes to describe them. For instance, a brilliantly colored autumn leaf "is a dazzling magic carpet." A flat, glossy shell might be "as smooth as a quiet, meandering river." Remember: a simile uses *like* or *as*; a metaphor does not. Write your similes and metaphors underneath each item.

5. On another part of the cardboard, use a Venn diagram to compare and contrast two objects. When you compare, state how the objects are alike; when you contrast, show their differences. Remember to use rich language!

6. Now, go off by yourself into a corner or special place at home or in your classroom. Daydream a little. What would you do all day in a cocoon? Could you live like a beetle under a rock? Hmmmm . . .

       0-7682-3125-6 *Creative Reading*

# Dancing Feet

**Materials:** dance videotape, pen or pencil, recorded music

**Directions:**

1. Watch a videotape borrowed from the library or one that you have with any kind of dancing. A good example is *The Nutcracker*, the classic ballet danced to music by Peter Tchaikovsky.

2. As you watch the various dances, listen to the mood or tone created by the music. Watch the choreography of the dancers. (*Choreography* means the movements and steps of the dancers.) Does the dancing fit the music's mood? How important is the music and the choreography to creating the mood of the dance?

3. Choose one of the dances you watched. Use the space below to use words or pictures to show the mood created by the music and the dance.

| Dance or Music Name | Mood Created by Music and Dance |
|---|---|
|  |  |

4. When you are finished looking at other people's dances, try choreographing your own! You may use recorded music to accompany your dance, or you may hum or sing your own music. Remember that the music should complement the mood of your dance. Have a friend use words or pictures to tell what mood they saw in your dance.

Published by Frank Schaffer Publications. Copyright protected.      0-7682-3125-6 *Creative Reading*

# Sound Off!

**Materials:** tape recorder

**Directions:**

1. Begin this activity with a moment of silence. What sounds do your students hear? Would they hear these sounds without intentionally listening? After you discuss various types of sounds, read aloud the passage below.

   > Your alarm clock RINGS and the bacon SIZZLES. Your bedroom door SLAMS and a garage door CREAKS open. The cat MEOWS and the dog BARKS! The birds TWITTER and the cars VRROOM! You might hear these sounds every morning. Maybe you don't even notice them! Yet, paying attention to sounds makes us more aware of the world around us.

2. Divide your students into two teams. Each team will use the tape recorder to record various sounds. Be sure they are in a private area so the other team doesn't hear them making the recording.

3. Each person on the team should record about three sounds. Instruct the class to make obvious sounds, such as a dog barking or a cat purring. Tell your students to use their imaginations (and their mouths!) as well, to make sounds such as the rain falling, a faucet dripping, or a computer keyboard clacking away.

4. When the recording is finished, play back the sounds. See if each team can recognize the sounds made by the other team.

5. Have a group discussion on how the sounds are alike and how they are different. Your students might be surprised at the similarities and differences. Rain splattering can sound like children running on a pavement. The ocean can sound like a kitchen faucet. What other noises are alike? What other noises are obviously different?

Grrrr    Hissss

0-7682-3125-6 *Creative Reading*

# Outside, Inside

**Materials:** a place in nature, notebook journal, camera or
markers and colored pencils

## Directions:

1. Sometimes feeling close to nature makes us feel better.
   Pick a place in your back yard, park, or anywhere
   outside where you feel comfortable. If you are away
   from home, have an adult with you.

2. Observe your nature spot over a six-week period. Visit
   once a week or more.

3. Each time you visit, write about how the plant and animal life changed from week to week
   and how it stayed the same. You can begin to record your thoughts on the lines below. Or
   you may want to create your own nature journal with your observations.

4. In addition to noting plant and animal life, write how you feel coming to your nature spot.
   Did your mood change as the environment or weather changed?

5. Draw pictures or use your camera to show transformations of your special place. Add the
   pictures to your journal.

6. At the end of the six weeks, look at your journal. What stayed the same at your spot?
   What changes occurred? Did leaves fall and animals hibernate? Did brand new buds sprout
   and pink, slithery worms appear? How did the changes in nature affect what you were
   feeling? For your final journal entry, describe how this natural, outside world connected to
   your own inside, personal world.

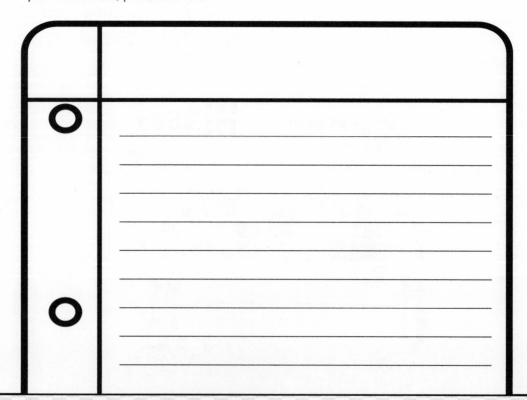

0-7682-3125-6 *Creative Reading*

# Just Add Milk

**Materials:** survey respondents and partners, cereal for research, empty cereal box, markers, construction paper, glue, video camera or tape recorder, various props, pen or pencil

**Directions:**

1. What would breakfast be without cereal? Do you like your cereal sugary sweet or wholesome and nutritious? Ask your family and friends what kind of cereal is their favorite. Compare and contrast their likes and dislikes.

| Name | Favorite Cereal | Why You Like It |
|---|---|---|
| | | |
| | | |
| | | |
| | | |

2. For a second survey, use the cereals you have at home or take a trip to the grocery store. Compare and contrast different kinds of cereals. How many grams of sugar do they have? Which ones have the most fiber? the most calories? Complete the table with any headings you choose: Fiber Calories, Grams of Sugar, Cost, or other qualities.

| Cereal Name | | |
|---|---|---|
| | | |
| | | |
| | | |
| | | |

3. Once you've done your research, create a new cereal. Make it from one or more of these grains: oats, wheat, rye, barley, rice, and corn. Will it have rice and nuts? Will it be chocolate flavored? Whether your new cereal is nutritious is up to you. Cover an empty box of cereal with construction paper and design a box for your cereal. With your partners, make a commercial for your new cereal using a video camera or a tape recorder.

# Pals Forever

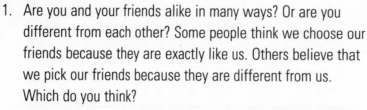

**Materials:** tape recorder, musical instrument (optional)

**Directions:**

1. Are you and your friends alike in many ways? Or are you different from each other? Some people think we choose our friends because they are exactly like us. Others believe that we pick our friends because they are different from us. Which do you think?

2. Think about your personality. Now, compare and contrast your personality to the personalities of your friends.
   - How are your personalities similar? How are they different?
   - What kinds of things do you like to do? Do your friends share the same interests? Or do they spend their free time doing completely different activities than you?
   - If you and your friend are quite different, what makes the friendship work?

3. After you've thought this through, write song lyrics or words that describe how you and your friends are the same and how you are different. You can use the Venn diagram below to get started with some words you could use for your song.

4. If you can read music, make up your own tune on any instrument you want. If you don't read music, use the tune to a song you already know.

5. Record your song for your friends and play it in their honor or sing it live!

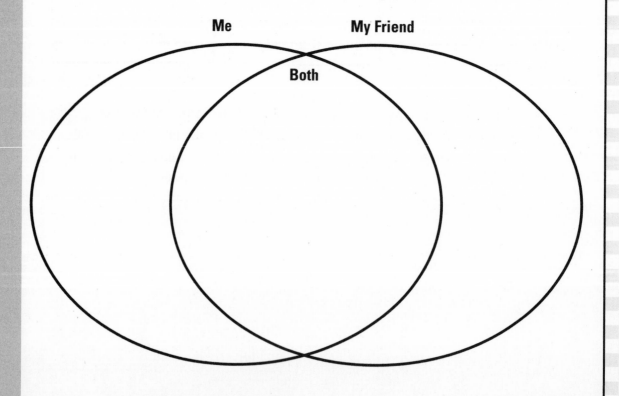

**Me**          **My Friend**

**Both**

0-7682-3125-6 *Creative Reading*

# What Would You Be?

**Materials:** survey respondents, pen or pencil

**Directions:**

1. There are millions of animals in the rain forests and other parts of the world. If you could be one animal, what would you be and why? Chart your answer below.

2. Then interview your friends and family members about what animals they would be. Ask them to explain their choices. Use the chart below to record their answers.

3. What do you notice about the relationship of someone's personality and the animal chosen? Did quiet people pick butterflies? Did talkative friends select howling monkeys? Did anyone opt for a roaring lion or a playful kitten?

4. Compare the personality of the human beings with the animals they chose. How are they the same?

5. After you've done that, contrast the personality of the people to the animals they chose. How are they different?

6. Did you learn anything about your friends and family members?

| Name | Animal Chosen | Why | Compare | Contrast |
|---|---|---|---|---|
| Me | | | | |
| | | | | |
| | | | | |
| | | | | |

       0-7682-3125-6 *Creative Reading*

# TV or Not TV!

**Materials:** large chart, markers, tape recorder or video camera, paper, pencils, online research or library books, various props (optional)

## Directions:

1. Begin this activity with a discussion on the broadcast media. Ask your students whether they like watching television more than they like listening to the radio.

2. Use a large chart to compare and contrast radio and TV. Does television lend itself to certain types of broadcasting? Is radio a medium that lets people use their imagination more? Would the students rather see a concert on TV than listen to it on the radio? Are there any differences between commercials on TV and those on the radio? Are there similarities? Are words and sounds more crucial to radio? How essential are facial expressions on TV? Ask any other questions that will spark your students to think about how radio and television are the same and how they are different.

3. Once your discussion is complete, divide your class into small groups, with six students as the maximum. Place the groups into either a "TV" or "Radio" category. Let each group choose a topic that matters to them. It can range from something that's in the news to a favorite food or anything that interests your students. Have your students do some research and note taking on their subjects.

4. Review the information on the TV/Radio chart you made. Then, based on their notes, have the students write short scripts on their topics. Remind the students to write their scripts with their medium in mind. For instance, the radio groups should rely on creating images with their words and sounds; the visual presentations by the television groups should be extensions of their written words.

5. When the students have finished writing their scripts, they will present their topics on the TV and radio evening news programs. You will tape record or videotape your students' presentations. Emphasize that the presentations should be collaborative efforts. Since the groups are small, each student should be able to be "On the Air" in some manner.

0-7682-3125-6 *Creative Reading*

# Take a Spin

**Materials:** construction paper, large piece of cardboard for spinning game board, fastener, markers, timer

**Directions:** Teaching students about cause and effect is a lot like teaching a code of ethics. In a nutshell, students must learn they are responsible for their actions because their actions have consequences. This activity allows you to blend the cause and effect found in literature with the cause and effect found in behavior and ethics.

1. First, think of thirty cause/effect situations you'd like to include. For example, a cause could be, "I helped at the bake sale," and the effect could be, "I raised money for the animal shelter." Another cause: "I spread a lie about someone"; the effect: "I hurt her reputation." You may tailor the actions and consequences to specific behavior that is occurring in your classroom.

2. Once you've determined your actions and consequences, make a round spinning game board out of cardboard, and divide it into thirty segments. Write one cause or action on each segment. Fasten a spinning arrow in the center. Mark each consequence on a piece of construction paper with bold markers so the students can easily read them. Spread the consequences face up on the floor.

3. To play: Set the timer for one minute. One student at a time spins the board. When the arrow stops on an action, the player reads the action aloud and then finds its consequence on the floor. When the player finds the consequence, he or she recites it aloud and puts it off to the side. The player then has whatever time remains on the timer to spin again and find another action/consequence setting. The player's turn is over when the timer dings. Then, it's the next person's chance to play. Who can find the most cause/effect circumstances in sixty seconds?

4. You may want to make up more than thirty cause/effect scenarios, depending on the size of your class. Or, you may have two smaller game boards so your class can play two games simultaneously. You may also use this concept for other cause/effect situations not tied to behavior and ethics.

0-7682-3125-6 *Creative Reading*

**Name** _____  **Date** _____

# Naturally

**Materials:** binoculars, magnifying glass, notebook journal, pen or pencil, magazines, scissors, glue

**Directions:** The world of nature never stands still. One event spawns another. In the world of literature, this is cause and effect. In nature, this is everyday life.

In stories, you can sometimes fix a difficult cause and effect. For example, if a character gets a flat tire on his bike (cause) and is late for a movie (effect), he can always go to a later showing of the film. In nature, it's not so easy to undo something or to remedy the cause and effect. For instance, if a moth flies too close to the spider's web and gets stuck (cause), the spider has a lovely dinner (effect). No chance to fix that one! Or if a hurricane's winds rage at 195 miles an hour (cause), a Florida town is devastated (effect).

Go outside. Look for natural episodes that show one thing causing something else to happen. It could be a gentle rain that waters the flowers. Or it could be a thundering rainstorm that sparks a blackout. Jot down your observations in the space below or in a journal. Add some drawings to show the cause and effect. If you can't go outside, cut out cause and effect pictures from the natural world from old magazines and glue them in your journal.

0-7682-3125-6 _Creative Reading_

# And Then . . . .

**Materials:** partners, index cards, pens or pencils

**Directions:** Every day you take actions that may lead to specific consequences. Actions cause consequences to happen. For example, if you leave your shoes outside in a rainstorm (action), they will get wet (consequence). In writing, this device is called *cause and effect*.

1. Think of one sentence that is an action sentence. It should contain a specific action.

2. Then think of a second sentence that contains a consequence. For instance, "The temperature dropped below freezing. We went ice skating on the pond."

3. Write each sentence on an index card.

4. Place your "action sentences" in one pile. Place your "consequence" sentences in another pile.

5. To play: Pick a card from each pile and see if you have a match. A match is when one of your cards has an action sentence and the other card contains the consequence that would occur.

6. If you have a match, act it out in pantomime. In pantomime, actors don't speak. They use gestures and facial expressions to act out their stories. Can your partners guess what you're acting out?

7. If you feel you don't have a match, put back both cards on the bottom of the pile. If you pick an action or consequence that you wrote, excuse yourself from guessing for this turn.

8. End the game when you've finished pairing up all the actions and consequences.

9. When you've gone through all of the cards several times, make a new set of action/consequence sets by writing new sentences.

10. A variation on this game is to draw the actions/consequences and have partners guess what you are showing.

# WHEEE!!

**Materials:** survey respondents, various items such as plastic building bricks, small plastic fruit baskets, pipe cleaners, modeling dough (recipe on page 96), small plastic people, small piece of poster board, makers

**Directions:** Amusement park rides always seem to attract us. They make us afraid, silly, nervous, anxious, brave, and, yes, even happy. Especially when they're over!

Ask your friends and family how amusement park rides make them feel. Ask them what parts of the rides make them feel certain ways. Does standing in line make them nervous? Does going up and over in loops make them afraid? Does going down a steep slope make them scream? Maybe hanging upside down makes them feel brave! Or does it make them feel silly? Does the ride's ending make them happy?

Use this chart to record the answers. Then, based on those answers, create an amusement park ride that includes all the feelings expressed by your friends and family. Make a sign out of poster board that will tout your ride's thrilling features. Maybe someday, you will design this ride for a real amusement park! WHEEE!!

| Name | What the Ride Does | How It Makes You Feel |
|------|--------------------|-----------------------|
|      |                    |                       |
|      |                    |                       |
|      |                    |                       |
|      |                    |                       |
|      |                    |                       |
|      |                    |                       |

0-7682-3125-6 *Creative Reading*

# How Did That Happen?

**Materials:** tape recorder, partners (optional)

**Directions:** Have you read the work of English author Rudyard Kipling? One of the best-known short stories by this Nobel Prize winner is "How the Camel Got His Hump." This delightful tall tale describes the arrogant ways of a camel and the consequences of his actions. Another term for actions and consequences is cause and effect. Something happens and that causes something else to happen.

1. It's your turn to spin your own yarn (that's another word for story). Before you begin writing, think about a question from nature you would like answered. Kipling's story answered the question, "How did the camel get his hump?" Use your daydreaming skills! Ever wonder how swans got such long necks? Or why spiders have eight legs? Whip up your own explanations!

2. The only two rules for the story are that it must have a cause and effect and it must be in the world of nature.

3. Once you are finished writing, narrate your story and record it.

4. Play the tape back while you act out your tall tale.

5. If you need to, ask some friends to play other parts. For more fun, use construction paper to make simple masks for the actors.

6. To learn more about Mr. Kipling, look for his *Just So Stories* and other books, tapes, and videos in the library.

# THUD!

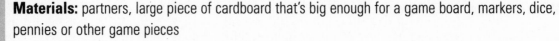

**Materials:** partners, large piece of cardboard that's big enough for a game board, markers, dice, pennies or other game pieces

**Directions:**

1. Create a game board with "Start" and "Finish" squares and about twelve zigzagging squares in between.

2. Write the name of one sound on each individual square. Each square should have a different sound. Use your imagination to conjure up interesting, zany, and even weird sounds. Make sure your sounds are realistic noises a person would hear.

3. To play: Roll the dice and move your game piece the number of spaces that you roll.

4. When you land on a sound, you must make up a sentence that can be a cause of that sound. For example, let's say you land on THUD! Your sentence could be, "I had a scary dream and fell out of bed." You can either say your sentence out loud or write it down.

5. Even if your sound is nutty, think of logical situations or events that would cause that sound. If you can't think of a sentence, you lose your next turn.

6. The winner is the first person to cross the finish line.

0-7682-3125-6 _Creative Reading_

# Home on the Biome

**Materials:** pen or pencil, shoebox, plastic plants, animals, or insects, sand, or soil (depending on the biome you choose), video camera (optional)

**Directions:** *Biomes* exist all over our vast planet. They are environments that have climates, plants, and animals that are specific to that region. Different biomes and climates can make us feel different ways.

The column on the left lists some biomes. The column on the right shows how those biomes would affect you. Match each biome to the way you would feel if you were there.

Next you will make a biome diorama out of a shoebox. You may use one of the biomes listed below, or any other biome. If you have a video camera, give a tour of your biome and describe how it feels to live there.

If you feel extra creative and ambitious, recreate your biome "out of the box" of your diorama. You could transform your room into a tropical rain forest or an icy tundra!

| | |
|---|---|
| desert | freezing |
| rain forest | amazed at the beautiful clear waters |
| cave | thirsty |
| scrub | hot and steamy |
| tundra | annoyed by a sharp prick from a shrub |
| coral reef | scary and dark |

**Name** _____ **Date** _____

# Twirl, Twist, Twine!

**Materials:** pencil or pen, tape recorder

**Directions:** No one can resist trying to say a tongue twister. You've probably twisted your own tongue a few times! See how you do with this one:

Mr. See owned a saw.
And Mr. Soar owned a seesaw.
Now See's saw sawed Soar's seesaw
Before Soar saw See,
Which made Soar sore.
Had Soar seen See's saw
Before See sawed Soar's seesaw,
See's saw would not have sawed
Soar's seesaw.
So See's saw sawed Soar's seesaw.
But it was sad to see Soar so sore
Just because See's saw sawed
Soar's seesaw!

In this tongue twister, the actions of Mr. See caused unpleasant consequences for Mr. Soar. If you think it's easy to twist the English language, try it. But we'll add an extra twist—no pun intended! Use Mr. See and Mr. Soar as your inspiration. Twine a tongue twister based on at least one action that sets off a consequence. Then, record your family and friends attempting to recite your tongue twister. Be prepared for a barrel of laughs!

_____

_____

_____

_____

_____

_____

_____

_____

_____

_____

0-7682-3125-6 *Creative Reading*

# Play Ball!

**Materials:** partners, a ball and any other sporting gear required, paper and pencil

**Directions:** In every sport, one action causes a consequence. Something happens which makes something else happen. The skater twists and turns on the rink, etching a figure eight into the ice. A football player throws a flawless pass to his teammate to score the winning touchdown. The bowling ball scoots down the center of the alley, scattering pins in every direction. The runner swiftly hands the baton to her teammate and spurs the team on to win the relay race.

1. Today you will think about actions and consequences to help you create a new sport. It can have any rules and procedures you like. However, you must use some kind of ball for your sport. In addition, your sport must have actions that spark consequences. Here's an example:

   - A player from each team begins at the starting line. The first objective is to throw a tennis ball into a bushel from fifteen feet away. Each player tries until this is accomplished.
   - When the ball lands in the basket, a second team member hops one hundred feet on one foot towards a third teammate.
   - When the hopping player reaches the teammate, that teammate walks toward the finish line balancing a tennis ball on a racket.
   - The first team to reach the finish line wins!

2. Describe your new sport and its rules. Be sure you include enough detail so anyone would be able to play it based on what you have written. Who knows? You just might create a new national pastime!

0-7682-3125-6 *Creative Reading*

# Can You Prove It?

**Materials:** notepad, pen or pencil

**Directions:** Arm yourself with a journal or notepad (or use the space below). This task will take some time and patience, but in the end, you will find it entertaining!

Everyone is entitled to an opinion. Yet, we often make an opinion look like a fact. You might have a friendly argument about who the best baseball player is. Let's say you have a favorite player in the major leagues. He doesn't have the best statistics. But for some reason, he is still your favorite player. During a talk with your friend, you blurt out, "Well, he's just as good as Babe Ruth was!" Is this a fact or an opinion?

For one week, every time you catch yourself disguising your opinion as fact, tally it up! Then, record the "Facts versus Opinions" for family members and friends. Did you run out of room in your notepad?

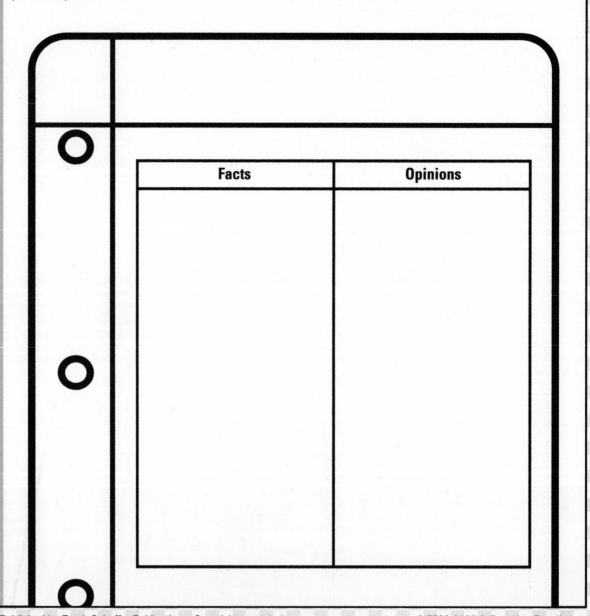

| Facts | Opinions |
|-------|----------|
|       |          |

0-7682-3125-6 *Creative Reading*

# Use It Again

**Materials:** trip to local recycling center, pencil, poster board, colored pencils or markers, magazines, glue, scissors, tape, recyclable objects, permission from your teacher to display recycle poster

**Directions:**

1. Call the local recycling center in your town. Ask if you can visit it and interview someone there.

2. Once you have arranged your visit, go with an adult. Get the facts about recycling in your town.
   - What can you recycle?
   - When are recycling days?
   - How does recycling help the environment?
   - How many tons of recycling material does your town produce a year?

3. Make a poster with all the facts you have learned. Draw pictures of recyclables or use pictures from magazines. If you want, fasten some small recyclables to the poster.

4. Now, pretend you are the planet Earth. Write some comments about how you feel when people recycle. State your opinions why people should recycle more. Ask your teacher if you can hang the recycle poster in your classroom.

0-7682-3125-6 *Creative Reading*

# Friendly Argument

**Materials:** newspaper and magazine articles, index cards, pens or pencils

**Directions:** At one time or another, everyone confuses facts with opinions. Sometimes, we are so passionate about a topic that we slip in a few opinions instead of relying on facts.

1. Have your students read newspaper and magazine articles. Suggest that they watch some news shows with an adult. Can they tell which members of the media spell out the facts and which try to sway the audience with opinions? Show your class the editorial and opinion pages of your local newspapers. Do they see the difference between the content on these pages and front-page news stories?

2. One of the best ways to act out the difference between facts and opinions is to hold debates. Let your class vote on a topic. It can range from a school-related issue to one that concerns the world. Less homework? Stricter pollution laws? A shorter school day? Watch as much TV as you want?

3. Start by creating two teams, with a maximum of six students on each team. The remainder of the students will be the judges. When the students finish debating, they will take their turns as judges, and the students who were judges will become debaters. The object of the debaters is to convince the judges that their team is right. The teams will be Pro or Con. You decide who will be on each team and which team will use only facts and which will use only opinions. For instance, the Pro team will rely solely on the facts to prove its case, while the Con team will depend on opinions to prove its point. All team members will debate.

4. Have your students research their topic before the debate. Research may range from online exploration to informal polls. Explain to your students they should put notes on index cards for effective speaking. Stress that if your students are "Fact" debaters, they cannot express their opinions during the debate. If they are "Opinion" debaters, they must avoid the facts.

5. Devise a scoring system for judges. For example, students may receive points for not deviating from the "Fact/Opinion" position, or they may lose points for personally criticizing an opponent's comments during the debate. The team with the highest score wins the debate. Let the debates begin!

0-7682-3125-6 *Creative Reading*

# Hot Off the Press!

**Materials:** newspapers, writing paper, pens or pencils, various art supplies

**Directions:** Show your students how newspapers are paradigms of facts and opinions. Students can learn fact and opinion from the inside out as they create a class newspaper.

1. Begin your newspaper planning with a brainstorming session for topics of interest to your budding journalists. Topics can range from what is happening in the world to what is happening in the classroom.

2. Before any writing happens, let your students see there are different ways to express facts and opinions within a newspaper. The more traditional examples are front-page news articles, editorials, and book reviews. However, show your students they can use facts to create crossword puzzles, mazes, and word jumbles. A sketch or photograph can illuminate an opinion, or conversely, it can point out the facts. Cartoon strips, jokes, and poems can easily voice opinions.

3. Let your students choose which types of pieces they want to work on. Try to have the paper evenly divided between examples of facts and opinions. The newspaper doesn't have to be fancy; handwritten or computer-typed articles stapled together will work! The focus here is substance and content, not appearance!

4. When the first edition is completed, use it as your class's paradigm to show the distinctions between facts and opinions.

5. You may want to extend this activity by reading a short biography of Ben Franklin. The students will get a kick out of Ben's *Silence Dogood* letters and his *Poor Richard's Almanack*.

0-7682-3125-6 *Creative Reading*

**Name** _____        **Date** _____

# Away You Go!

**Materials:** encyclopedia or ability to do online research, markers or colored pencils, pen or pencil

## Directions:

1. Think of a country or state that would be a great place for an adventure. Research it and jot down four sightseeing activities you want to do while you are there on vacation. These activities will be the "facts" you use for advertising this place.

2. In the squares below, draw pictures that show you participating in these sightseeing activities. Are you nervous while you go whitewater rafting? Are you laughing as you ride the world's biggest roller coaster? Use thought bubbles to explain what you're thinking!

3. When you're done, express your opinion about whether or not this place would make a great vacation spot. Bon Voyage!

<table>
<tr><td></td><td></td></tr>
<tr><td></td><td></td></tr>
</table>

**My Opinion**

_____

_____

_____

0-7682-3125-6 *Creative Reading*

# Music to My Ears

**Materials:** drawing paper, markers or colored pencils, magazines, glue, scissors

**Directions:**

1. A famous musician has asked you to design a new kind of musical instrument. There's only one rule: it must be in the percussion family. A percussion instrument is one that makes a sound when you hit it. Drums, vibraphones, cymbals, triangles, bongos, wood blocks, and tambourines are all percussion instruments.

2. To design this instrument, you may use parts or concepts from existing percussion instruments. Or, you may dream up something totally different. When you've designed your instrument, create an ad on drawing paper for a magazine or newspaper. Your ad must state these facts:

   - that the instrument is a percussion instrument
   - the sound or sounds the instrument makes
   - how much it will cost
   - the materials used to make the instrument
   - what kind of music is best for this instrument (You might want to use this instrument for all music types, or only for one kind, such as rock.)
   - how long it takes to make one instrument

3. Once you state the facts, quote some fictional musicians in your ad. (You can use pictures of people in magazines as your famous musicians.) These musicians should state their opinions about why this is the best musical instrument ever invented! Their opinions should convince people to buy this instrument. Who knows? The most famous musicians in the world may wind up playing your new instrument!

0-7682-3125-6 *Creative Reading*

# Tribute

**Materials:** various items, especially natural elements (such as wood, plants, rocks, shells, sand, tree bark), modeling dough (recipe on page 96), poster board, markers, pen or pencil

**Directions:** You could spend years visiting all the monuments, statues, and memorials that dot our cities and landscapes. And, it's safe to say that you will never ever forget any of them. Places such as Mount Rushmore or the Statue of Liberty will touch you and make you think.

1. Design a place of honor that celebrates what is important to you. It may represent a concept such as freedom. Or it may depict a person you admire. Your model will be a replica of the real-life version.

2. Use manmade supplies such as clay to begin with, but focus on natural materials to construct your final model. See what you can find outside. Let these materials show the spirit of the concept or person you chose.

3. When you are done, create a plaque out of poster board. List some facts about your creation.
   - What did you use to make it?
   - Where will it be located?
   - How big will the real-life version be?
   - Then, give your opinion about why this tribute is valid.
   - Make a visitor see why this concept or person should be valued and honored.

0-7682-3125-6 *Creative Reading*

# Help Is on the Way!

**Materials:** markers or colored pencils, poster board

**Directions:** Read the three paragraphs below. Each factual passage describes an event that needs volunteers. After you read each paragraph, decide which activity you would want to attend. The passages state facts, but you have to decide which event, in your opinion, would be best for you. Create a poster for that activity that will draw other students to it. On the poster, speak out! Express your opinions to show what someone will get out of the activity or how you think it will make them feel.

1. There will be a car wash on Saturday, October 9. Proceeds from the car wash will benefit the Maple Avenue Animal Shelter at 55 Maple Avenue. We want more people to know about the shelter. Our goal is to raise money so we can advertise it. We also want to take good care of the animals while they are here. We need all hands to wash, scrub, and vacuum dirty autos! Let's help our furry friends find permanent homes! See you at 9 A.M.!

2. Maple Avenue Middle School needs you! Join us for an afternoon of rollerskating at the Rollerama, 32 Beech Street, October 10, 1:00 P.M. Bring two or three food items that won't spoil. Our school will donate these items to families who need them. In addition, the Rollerama has agreed to donate proceeds from all admission tickets to our local food pantry. See you there!

3. Delicious donations! Maple Avenue's fifth grade will hold a bake sale on Saturday, October 2, in Maple Park. All donations will pay for the class trip to the aquarium. Help bake, help sell, and help eat! Bake sale time is from 10 A.M. until 3 P.M.

After you've chosen your activity and made a poster, see if there is any way that you can use that idea for a real-life activity of your own. Remember to involve an adult.

# You Get the Picture!

**Materials:** pen or pencil, drawing paper, paint brushes, water colors, acrylic paints, markers or colored pencils

**Directions:** For this three-step activity, you must look deep inside yourself.

1. On the lines below, state physical facts about yourself. What color are your eyes and hair? Are you tall or short? Do you have a big smile? You get the picture.

| The Facts |
|---|
|  |
|  |
|  |
|  |

2. Once you've listed your physical facts, think about your personality. How do you view yourself? Do you like who you are? Do you think of yourself as a kind person? Do you think that you could be nicer? State your opinions about yourself.

| My Opinion of Myself |
|---|
|  |
|  |
|  |
|  |

3. Now comes the tricky part. Draw a self-portrait that portrays the facts about your physical self. This drawing, however, must also get across your opinions about your character. Let this drawing reveal who you are. Or, who you think you are! Some people think all great art speaks the truth. Do you think that, too?

_____

_____

_____

0-7682-3125-6 *Creative Reading*

# Good Morning

**Directions:**

1. Read the passage below. The author writes this passage to describe how she feels one particular morning.

2. When you are finished reading, think about the scene. What is the author feeling?

3. Create a dance (alone or with a partner) that interprets the scene and shows the author's emotions. Pay close attention to where the author is. Portray that place in your dance, too, and make it come alive!

The water, tinged with pink and blue, goes on forever. I stand before infinity in awe of Mother Nature's beauty. Wave after wave rolls in, quietly, as if the water is not up yet. It is early, when most everyone is still asleep. For me, this is the best time to be here, before the crowds and noises come. It is best to be here, I think, before other footprints sink into the sand. It is best to be here when I am captivated by sand crabs dancing along the shore. Or when the only sounds I hear are the caws of stark white gulls calling to each other. It is best to be here when I feel so free and alive that I can run, and there is no one to catch me!

The sun rises slowly, as if it wants me to coax it into the sky. I chuckle at its playfulness! I feel so alive here, so full of wonder at the universe! It is hard to imagine that anything else exists. Is it true there are video games and cities and tiny telephones? No, that can't be!

# What's Behind This?

**Directions:** On page 81, there is a passage titled "Fairy Floss." The readers must decipher what the author is talking about by looking at sentence clues. A puzzle within the activity connects it to the logical/mathematical intelligence. The student solves the brainteaser by answering questions about the piece.

All of the questions relate to the author's purpose reading skill. Why and how an author writes something can be as important, if not more important, than what is written. Understanding the nuance of language and literary devices used by writers will enhance your fifth graders' reading skills and comprehension. Delving into author's purpose passages is an excellent opportunity for your students to use their inferential, organizational, and reasoning skills.

1. To prepare for this activity, discuss the difference between a metaphor and a simile. Here's an easy way for your students to remember what a simile is: Similes normally use *like* and *as*. Point out that the word *simile* has an *l* for *like*, and an *s* for *as*. If your students can remember this, they will also remember that a metaphor (no *s* or *l*) is the comparison that does not use *like* or *as*. Have the students use items in the classroom to make metaphor/simile comparisons.

2. Read short magazine or newspaper articles and ask your students why the authors wrote them. Ask them why the authors used a simile or a metaphor. Ask them what the author means by a particular sentence. Can they understand the author's meaning through inference?

3. The "Fairy Floss" passage also asks a question about first, second, or third person. Discuss these points of view with your students and ask them which one they prefer to read. Does it depend on the genre they are reading? Which point of view do they prefer to use as an author?

4. The passage also asks a question about senses. Explain that authors like to use sense images in their writing. They can add a thoughtful, enriching dimension to almost any piece. Expand this concept and have your students write poems about their favorite senses. If they'd rather, have them act out their favorite senses, or dance them. The students can even write a song about how they love to taste pizza. You could have a "Sense-ational Day" when the entire curriculum revolves around the five senses and how writers use them in their works.

0-7682-3125-6 *Creative Reading*

**Author's Purpose**

# Fairy Floss

**Directions:** After you read this mystery passage, answer the questions. Write the jumbled answer letters on the lines below and unscramble them. What is Fairy Floss?

To the Australians, it is Fairy Floss. It looks as delicate as a spider's web. It's possible that slaves in ancient Rome first made this, but no one is sure of that. Many other sweet things, and some soaps, also possess its main ingredient. Our mystery item feels weird, smells divine, and tastes delicious. Unless you want a vanishing act, don't ever put it in water! And, if you ever make it, don't let it spin out of control!

**1. and 7.**    When the author says "it is Fairy Floss," she uses—

        C.  a metaphor.

        D.  a simile.

        E.  a preposition.

**2. and 5.**    "It looks as delicate as a spider's web" is a—

        N.  metaphor.

        O.  simile.

        P.  main idea.

**3. and 4.**    The main ingredient is—

        T.  sugar.

        U. a potato.

        V. also used to make keys.

**6. and 9.**    Why did the author write this?

        L. to discuss ancient Rome

        M. to explain how soap is made

        N. to describe a mystery item

**8.**    This story is written in the

        A. third person

        B. second person

        C. first person

**10.**    Four senses describe Fairy Floss. Name the missing fifth sense.

        B. sight

        C. smell

        D. hearing

**11.**    What will happen if you put the mystery item in water?

        X. It will grow.

        Y. It will disappear.

        Z. It will freeze.

__6__ __4__ __1__ __3__ __8__ __10__ __11__ __5__ __7__ __9__ __2__

# Listen to This

**Materials:** radio, or CDs and player, pen or pencil

**Directions:** Listen to six songs with lyrics. There is always a reason an artist creates a work of art. On the chart below, list why you think the artists crafted these pieces. Did they want you to feel sad or happy? Was the purpose to tell a story about friendship or love? Then, pretend you're the musician. Keep in mind the musician's message, but give the piece a different title. Whose title do you like better? Why?

| Song Name | Why Created? | Your New Title |
|---|---|---|
|  |  |  |
|  |  |  |
|  |  |  |
|  |  |  |
|  |  |  |
|  |  |  |

# Dear Journal

**Materials:** notebook journal, pen or pencil, trip to pet store or zoo

**Directions:** Read the paragraph below.

There's no place I'd rather live than here. Life in this beautiful Mexican rain forest is superb. In fact, it's warm and splendid. Oh, let me introduce myself. I am an agouti. "A what?" you might ask. I realize I'm not the most well-known animal in the world, but I am worth getting to know. An agouti is a rodent. I have tiny ears and a one-inch tail. I'd prefer a tail as long a lemur's, but Mother Nature thought otherwise. I'm not the most beautiful animal in the rain forest, either. My fur is brown and bristly. My body is chunky, with long legs that make me a swift runner. Believe me, those legs come in handy when an anaconda is hunting me down for its dinner. When you are the prey, you feel petrified and lonely. Anacondas are my worst enemy. They frighten me. They're sneaky when they wait in the swamps for me to come by, but don't worry: there's no way this agouti will be a meal for one of those squeezers. Speaking of meal, I've got to get my own dinner. I'm famished, and it's about time I gathered up some seeds and roots, although fruit would be nice, too.

1. Why did the author write this piece from the point of view of an agouti? She wanted to teach you about this mammal, but she also wanted you to feel like it, too.

2. Take a trip to the zoo or a pet store. Observe one animal there. Watch its habits and how it reacts to the other animals and you. Maybe, it won't even notice you!

3. Once you are back home, pretend you are that animal. In your journal, explain two things: how it would feel to be that animal and how your experiences relate to those of the animal. For instance, if you said you felt the animal looked frightened, describe a time when you were afraid. If your animal looks happy and content, explain what makes you happy. If your animal feels proud and bold, give examples of how you have felt that same way, too.

4. In this journal entry, your purpose is to describe the experiences of two animals: one that you'll never become, and one that you already are.

**Author's Purpose**

# ♫ Snap to It

**Materials:** partner, tape recorder, your body to make sounds

**Directions:**

1. Look through a book of poetry and choose a poem you like. Think hard about why the author wrote this poem.
   - What is the mood of the poem?
   - How was the author feeling when he or she wrote this poem?
   - How did he or she want you to feel?
   - What main message was the author trying to convey?

2. Discuss the poem with your partner. Answer all of the questions above and make additional comments. Once you understand why the author wrote the poem and what it means, try this activity.

3. Put on your tape recorder. You or your partner will take turns reciting the poem. The other person will make sounds that connect to the poem. There's a catch, though! The only instrument you'll have for this activity is your body! Here are some things you might try:
   - whistle
   - tap your hands and feet
   - clap
   - snap your fingers
   - hum
   - sing softly in the background.
   You can tap out the beat of the poem or make sounds that are mentioned in the poem. Have your sounds connect to the rhythm that the author chose for this poem. Often, authors purposely relate the beat of the poem to its mood. Can you do the same?

4. Did you know that during the 1950s, a group of writers called beatniks invented a new way of clapping?
   They snapped their fingers to show their appreciation for poetry readings or concerts.

0-7682-3125-6 *Creative Reading*

# Some Day

**Materials:** writing paper, pens or pencils, tape recorder or video camera

**Directions:**

1. Biographies and autobiographies are powerful tools authors use to define either their lives or the lives of others. Explain the differences between an autobiography and a biography to your students. Take this further and point out what authorized and unauthorized biographies are.

2. This activity will combine the forces of nature, some poetic license, and your students' writing skills. Use the great outdoors to inspire your students. Even if your school is in an urban environment, there's still a piece of sky your students can see, or a warm spring breeze that can brush against their faces.

3. As you spend time outside, tell your students to daydream about the future they want to have. They may only be fifth graders, but more than likely, many of them are already envisioning the lives they'd like to lead.

4. When they are finished imagining and taking notes, have the students come back inside. The next step is for them to write their autobiographies based on their reflections. Take some poetic license, and let the students pretend they are in their eighties. They will write their autobiographies as first person narrative accounts, recounting the events as they occurred.

5. When the students are finished writing, make a video or tape recording of each child's autobiography. Let your students add music and sounds to their autobiographies. Encourage them to dance them or act them out. There aren't any boundaries here!

6. In addition to sharpening the author purpose skills of your students, this exercise will give you some invaluable insight into who your students are and who they want to become.

7. An additional twist on this exercise would be to have the students interview each other and then write biographies of their classmates. You can decide if they should be authorized or unauthorized!

# Meet the Critters

**Materials:** online research or library books, pen or pencil, paper, tape recorder

**Directions:**

1. You've become the host of a new radio show called "Meet the Critters." Since you love animals so much, this is your dream job! Every week, each show will highlight all the facts about one animal.
   - What does the animal eat?
   - Where does it live?
   - What does it look like?
   - What does it eat?
   - Does it have any natural predators?
   - Is it endangered?
   - Does the animal rely on any one sense for its survival?
   - What are its everyday habits?

2. Choose an animal that you don't know much about. Have you ever heard of a rabbit-eared bandicoot? How about a quokka? Research your guest critter online. Or, you may use library books. Give the listeners as many facts as possible.

3. When you finish gathering your data, record your information for your listeners. Your narration should be concise and to the point. Your voice is the only way your listeners will learn about this animal. Change your tone. Stress different words and be the picture for your listeners. Ask yourself this question: "Why am I reporting on this animal?" If you can answer that question clearly, you will be doing a great job!

0-7682-3125-6 *Creative Reading*

# Let Me Tell You!

**Materials:** various media, paper, large chart, markers, pens or pencils

**Directions:**

1. Give your students some background in expository, descriptive, and persuasive writing. The explanations should be short and simple: expository explains, descriptive describes, and persuasive persuades or convinces. Illustrate your point with book excerpts, poems, magazine pieces, and newspaper articles. Seeing examples of the various types of writing helps many students understand them better.

2. For this activity, concentrate on persuasive writing. Divide your class into small groups, with six students as the maximum. Let the students decide on their topics, or you may choose them to tie in with your curriculum.

3. The students must collaborate on writing one cohesive, persuasive essay. Through their essays, the students must convince the other students to agree with their points of view. For instance, let's say the students choose "Why living in warm weather is better than living in cold weather." This essay should make someone want to wear a bathing suit all year-round!

4. Have your students determine a persuasive essay rubric. The rubric should include key points the students feel a strong, convincing, persuasive essay should have.

5. Make a large chart with the rubric and use it to assess the various essays. When all the convincing is done, have the students act out their essays. Which essay was the most persuasive?

6. At another time, you may choose to divide your students into groups and have each group write an expository or descriptive essay.

**Name** _____                          **Date** _____

# New Species?

**Materials:** binoculars, magnifying glass, modeling dough (recipe on page 96), flower pot, dirt, sand, index card, pen or pencil

**Directions:** The world is filled with interesting and unusual species of plants. Did you know that the most colossal flower on the planet has a horrible smell? It's true! The rain forest's rafflesia flower smells like rotten, rancid meat! The rafflesia is three feet in diameter and weighing twenty pounds; its odor must be dreadful! Today's activity will allow you to learn more about some of the mysteries in nature (and come up with a new mystery of your own!).

1. Walk around your house or schoolyard or take a trip to a park with an adult. Use your binoculars and magnifying glass to look closely at the trees, plants, and flowers.
   - Which of these gifts from nature attract you?
   - Why do you like them?
   - Are you attracted to their smells?
   - Do their colors fascinate you?
   - Do you like their textures?
   - Do you like the way they look?
   - Are they eye-catching?

2. Now that you've taken your walk, write down the things you observed.

3. Use your observations (and your imagination!) to design a new flower, plant, or tree. Use modeling dough to fashion your new creation. You can even stick it in a flower pot filled with dirt or sand.

4. Concoct a name for your new species and write it on an index card. Insert some additional information on the card, too. Imagine your new species will be at a garden store and you are writing information for people who might buy it.
   - How does your flower smell?
   - How big will it grow?
   - Does it thrive in freezing weather?
   - Does it require sun?
   - How often do you need to water it?

0-7682-3125-6 _Creative Reading_

# Plant an Idea

**Directions:** Three pages in this reading skill section are devoted to one single idea—a tree (see pages 90–92). Students begin by illustrating a picture using a tree as the theme. They have free rein with their settings and characters, but their drawings must portray a plot that revolves around the tree. The artwork must demonstrate what is happening in the story and depict characters, settings, and plot. For a second activity, the students must write a fictional account based on their pictures. A third activity links the theater to the illustrations and fictional pieces.

1. Begin by sharing any well-illustrated books with your students. They will capture the essence of how good pictures help tell a story. A thoughtful, humorous, child-oriented cartoon strip will accomplish the same thing. Show them some of your favorite paintings or photographs. A picture may be worth a thousand words, but it can also inspire a thousand words!

2. Get your students to think about their story elements before they draw. Review character, plot, setting, and point of view in a simple manner. Explain the importance of dialogue in telling a story. This gently coaxes them to think in an organized and visual manner.

3. Ask your students to close their eyes and imagine a tree. This helps them create their settings. Explain that their illustrations must connect to the stories they tell. Randomly coloring a few flowers on the page does not tell a story that focuses on the tree. Show your students how the tree can be the basis and device for a plot revolving around a cat stuck in a tree. This event causes the whole town to rescue the cat. A more science fiction-minded student might say that the tree harbors a swarm of nasty bees ready to wreak havoc on the school.

4. This is a fictional exercise, yet it is a good time to point out that other reading skills, such as the main idea/details, cause/effect, author's purpose, sequencing, and summarizing, are also important in a fictional account.

5. After your students have their illustrations and writing done, they'll tie their stories into the musical and theatrical worlds.

6. This theme-related segment shows your students that creativity is a process. By drawing, writing, and acting, your students witness one concept serving as a catalyst for another and yet another.

# A Tree Grows Here!

**Materials:** markers or colored pencils, notebook journal, pen or pencil

**Directions:** Before you begin this activity, go outside. Look at every tree you can find. Observe the different kinds of bark, leaves, flowers, or fruits. Are there animals living in any of the trees? Do the trees appear healthy or sick? Are they rugged and strong or thin and willowy? Write down your observations. If you don't have any trees where you live, get a library book on trees and explore.

Now, draw a picture using the tree as the center of attention. Your setting or place (time, too) can be anywhere: city, country, schoolyard, rain forest, or an unknown planet! Put characters in your picture and have a plot that revolves around the tree. The plot, in simple terms, is the story behind the picture. Show the story through your artwork.

0-7682-3125-6 *Creative Reading*

# Write It!

**Materials:** pen or pencil

**Directions:** For this activity, you will need your illustration from page 90. Use that drawing to write a story that has a tree as its theme. Look at the details in your illustration. What story are you telling? Remember to explain your plot. Describe what your characters are doing and why. Include where your story takes place. Use dialogue for the words spoken by your characters. For instance, "I said, 'Where's my cat? Oh no, he's caught in the tree!'" Who is telling your story? Are you narrating it in first person or is someone else telling it?

_____

_____

_____

_____

_____

_____

_____

_____

_____

_____

_____

_____

_____

_____

_____

_____

_____

_____

_____

_____

_____

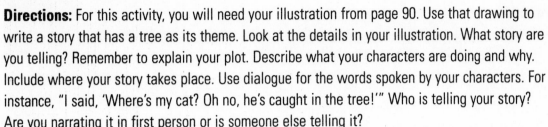

# Act It!

**Materials:** partners, props found at home or school, CD and player (optional)

**Directions:**

1. Use the story you wrote on page 91. Now it's time to take your act on the road! Transform your tree story into a musical, drama, or comedy.

2. Ask some friends to play the parts of your characters. You may want to have someone narrate the lines that are not dialogue.

3. If you are doing a drama or comedy, act out the lines. If you are presenting a musical, sing the lines. Use tunes you've made up or the melody to a song that you like. If you want, play background music that suits the tone or mood of your piece.

4. Make sure you project your voices and express the appropriate emotions. Nothing is more boring than an actor with a monotone voice!

5. Props are an important part of the setting, so choose your props wisely. You don't need many props, just enough to convey the atmosphere you want. Even major Broadway productions sometimes have very sparse settings!

6. Your theatrical piece can last as long as you need to tell the story.

0-7682-3125-6 *Creative Reading*

# What Would They Say?

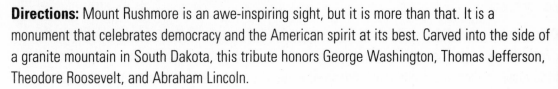

**Materials:** three other partners, pens or pencils

**Directions:** Mount Rushmore is an awe-inspiring sight, but it is more than that. It is a monument that celebrates democracy and the American spirit at its best. Carved into the side of a granite mountain in South Dakota, this tribute honors George Washington, Thomas Jefferson, Theodore Roosevelt, and Abraham Lincoln.

Pretend these men have come alive. Use the lines below to write a dialogue for these characters. Show how they would view the United States today. Each character must speak at least three lines. Now, act out the lines in a mini-play.

_____

_____

_____

_____

_____

_____

_____

_____

_____

_____

_____

_____

_____

_____

_____

# Happy? Sad?

**Materials:** small drum, oatmeal container, or anything that could substitute for a small drum, pen or pencil

**Directions:** Look at the six faces below. Can you tell how each character feels? Underneath each picture, write the emotion the character shows. That sounds too easy, so let's make it a little more challenging. Under each emotion, write a comment your character would say that shows the emotion he or she feels. For instance, a nervous character might say, "I know I did it last night, but now I can't find my homework!" Then, use your drum to tap out a beat that matches each character's emotion.

Published by Frank Schaffer Publications. Copyright protected.          0-7682-3125-6 *Creative Reading*

# Fabulous Fables

**Materials:** paper or large chart, pens or pencils, various materials for costumes (optional)

Directions: Most, if not all, fifth graders, can probably recite Aesop's tale of "The Hare and the Tortoise" by heart. What most students probably don't realize is how this fable, and many others, imparts morals and life lessons without being heavy-handed.

Fables are wonderful aspects of our literary world. They embody all the characteristics of a great work of fiction: rich language, succinct themes, identifiable characters, and settings that make us feel as if we are there. Add talking animals, and you have an excellent recipe for literature that grabs the attention of adults and students alike.

Read some fables to your students. Aesop's fables are a good place to start, but also look into the work of the seventeenth-century French writer, Jean de La Fontaine. Your students may find it interesting to know that in the dictionary, a "fabulist" is someone who creates or reads fables aloud. It is also described as someone who is a liar. Explain that fables have morals, and in simplest terms, morals teach us how to behave.

Once you have set the stage by reading the works of other fabulists, it will be the students' turns to create a fifth-grade fable. You may do this project together as a class, or you may divide your class into groups. If you do this as an ensemble project, you may want to write down the fable on a large chart. Remind your students that in a fable, animals are the main characters, and . . . they talk! Discuss with your students which animals might project certain personality traits. For instance, a lamb would easily represent a timid character, while a lion would best signify a bold and daring character. However, if the fabulists wanted to interject some humor, they could purposely choose a lion to symbolize a timid character, such as the cowardly lion in *The Wizard of Oz*.

Explain that fables must contain the main story elements of characters, place, plot, time, and point of view. When the fables are finished, have the students act them out. To add another dimension to this activity, let your students fashion their own animal costumes.

Verbal-Linguistic Intelligence

Logical-Mathematical Intelligence

Bodily-Kinesthetic Intelligence

Visual-Spatial Intelligence

Musical Intelligence

Interpersonal Intelligence

Intrapersonal Intelligence

Naturalist Intelligence

# Answer Key

The answers below are for those few pages that require specific responses. Since this is an *UnWorkbook*, concrete answers don't apply to the vast majority of the pages. However, as a general guide, look for this criteria to ensure your students are getting the most out of this book. Are they doing their best to think out of the box? move? create? make something? listen? explore? push the envelope? challenge themselves? stretch their imagination and themselves? have fun?

### Pine Cones, Sunflowers, and Infinity! ..............page 20

1,1,2,3,5,8,13,21,34,55,89 The Fibonacci pattern is based on a series of numbers.
1+1=2;1+2=3;3+2=5, and so on. The pattern progresses by adding the last two numbers to get the sum of the next number.

### Can You Guess? ..........................page 31

Seven

### Eight Letters to My Name.................................page 33

Envelope

### Think Straight! .............................page 36

Three clips go across the top. Four clips, from the top down, slant diagonally to the left. Three clips go across on the bottom. The letter Z is formed.

### Pack Up .........................................page 44

These items should be on the right hand side of the suitcase: scarf, knitted hat, mittens, parka, sweaters, collapsible ski poles, boots, woolen socks, snow suit. These items should be in the middle: flip flops, sun tan lotion, scuba gear, bathing suit.
These items should be on the far left: nice shoes and nice dress clothes. Carry-on bag could include shorts, sun glasses, tie, T-shirts, ski masks, and anything else the reader feels will be necessary.

### Home on the Biome ...................page 67

desert/thirsty
rain forest/hot and steamy
cave/scary and dark
scrub/annoyed by a sharp prick from a shrub
tundra/freezing
coral reef/amazed at the beautiful clear waters

### Fairy Floss .....................................page 81

1. C
2. O
3. T
4. T
5. O
6. N
7. C
8. A
9. N
10. D
11. Y

COTTON CANDY

### Happy? Sad? ...............................page 94

Answers may vary. Suggestions: angry, puzzled, nervous, happy or excited, sad, unsure or skeptical

### Modeling Dough Recipe

Adult supervision is required for making modeling dough.

Bring 2 cups (0.47 L) water to a boil. Add food coloring in the color of your choice. Mix together 2 ½ cups (592 mL) flour, 1 Tbs. (15 mL) powdered alum, ½ cup (118 mL) salt, and 3 Tbs. (45 mL) vegetable oil. Add the colored water to this mixture. Mix well and knead until soft. Store in an airtight container.

0-7682-3125-6 *Creative Reading*